Better Homes and Gardens®

roses

written by Eleanore Lewis

Better Homes and Gardens® Books
Des Moines, Iowa

Better Homes and Gardens® Books
An imprint of Meredith® Books

Roses
Writer: Eleanore Lewis
Editor and Project Manager: Kate Carter Frederick
Art Director: Lyne Neymeyer
Project Coordinator: Beth Ann Edwards
Research Coordinator: Rosemary Kautzky
Copy Chief: Terri Fredrickson
Book Production Managers: Pam Kvitne, Marjorie J. Schenkelberg
Contributing Copy Editor: Barbara Feller-Roth
Contributing Proofreaders: Kathy Roth Eastman, Fran Gardner,
    Tricia Toney
Illustrator: Tom Rosborough
Indexer: Jana Finnegan
Electronic Production Coordinator: Paula Forest
Editorial and Design Assistants: Kaye Chabot, Mary Lee Gavin,
    Karen Schirm

Meredith® Books
Editor in Chief: James D. Blume
Design Director: Matt Strelecki
Managing Editor: Gregory H. Kayko
Executive Editor, Gardening and Home Improvement:
    Benjamin W. Allen

Director, Sales, Special Markets: Rita McMullen
Director, Sales, Premiums: Michael A. Peterson
Director, Sales, Retail: Tom Wierzbicki
Director, Book Marketing: Brad Elmitt
Director, Operations: George A. Susral
Director, Production: Douglas M. Johnston

Better Homes and Gardens® Magazine
Editor in Chief: Karol DeWulf Nickell
Executive Garden Editor: Mark Kane

Meredith Publishing Group
President, Publishing Group: Stephen M. Lacy

Meredith Corporation
Chairman and Chief Executive Officer: William T. Kerr

Chairman of the Executive Committee: E. T. Meredith III

All of us at Better Homes and Gardens® Books are dedicated to
providing you with information and ideas to enhance your home
and garden. We welcome your comments and suggestions. Write to
us at: Better Homes and Gardens Books, Garden Editorial
Department, 1716 Locust St., Des Moines, IA 50309-3023.

If you would like to purchase any of our gardening, cooking, crafts,
home improvement, or home decorating and design books, check
wherever quality books are sold. Or visit us at: bhgbooks.com

Cover Photograph: 'Henri Martin' Moss rose by Charles Mann

roses

introduction

living history

Call them time travelers. Roses manage to do what we cannot: They defy age. Surviving through the ages, roses have been treasured by generations for their beauty as well as their colorful folklore. According to one Roman poet, "The rose was either born from a smile of Cupid or else it fell from the hair of Aurora." Ancient Greeks called the rose the "queen of flowers," and Homer referred to oil of roses in the *Iliad*. Nero supposedly showered his guests with thousands of rose petals. Roses appeared on coins as far back as 4000 B.C. in central Asia. The Chinese cultivated new varieties of roses centuries before explorers brought the first ones back to Europe in the 1700s. That's history!

Today, you can grow many of the old Heirloom varieties in your own garden, or opt for Modern hybrids, which offer a variety of characteristics from repeat blooming and disease resistance to compact growth and seemingly perfect flowers. Use roses in the garden as highlights, specimens, sources of fragrance, or problem-solvers. Let a rampant Climber disguise an unattractive building, or prevent erosion on a slope by planting groundcover roses.

In the end, gardeners always return to the most desirable features of roses–their essential beauty and fragrance–and breeders continue to work to enhance these qualities in their quest for new and better roses.

traditional beauty

right: **Two splendid Climbers demonstrate the irresistible appeal of growing roses, with their luscious blossoms and heady fragrance as well as the outstanding way they greet anyone at the door.**

specific wonders

left: Modern hybrids with single flowers imitate the simplicity of time-tested Species and other Old Garden roses. Single-petal roses never fail to astonish people with their simple beauty. Although Species roses grow too vigorously for confinement in a container or a traditional border, they make excellent specimens or hedge plants, especially in a naturalistic garden. Species roses represent the original, wild roses. Their durability ensures their success, as it has through the ages.

rescued heirlooms

left: Thanks to the intrepid people known as rose rustlers, many of the oldest roses left to obscurity have been brought back to home gardens. Rustlers persist in rescuing roses from neglected cemeteries and abandoned homesteads. With diligent research, they resurrect forgotten names of roses passed down through generations of gardeners. Having survived with a minimum of attention for decades, these Heirlooms are the ultimate in easy-care, hardy roses.

introduction

choosing your roses

Have fun with roses, no matter which kind you choose. Design a garden that includes roses from Empress Josephine's 19th-century garden at Malmaison, France, or roses with names that have special meaning for you and your family, or dates of introduction that coincide with family birthdays or anniversaries. If you don't already raise a memorable rose from your grandmother's garden, choose from dozens of varieties once popular among American pioneers, Victorians, and Depression-era gardeners, such as 'Harison's Yellow' and *Rosa gallica*. Look for the date of introduction listed (in parentheses) with the rose descriptions in "the roses" section that follows. Find varieties that match the vintage of your house, if you like, or roses with names that tickle your fancy.

On the practical side, consider your garden space, landscape style, and goals when you select roses. Roses grow in all shapes and sizes, with different bloom times and flower types. Some offer outstanding foliage; others boast disease resistance and superb hardiness. Roses climb, arch, and sprawl; they grow as compact and miniature gems as well as robust giants. On the following pages, you'll find dozens of suggestions for roses old and new that suit a variety of functions, designs, and climates. Making up your mind about which ones to grow in your garden will be the hardest part of joining in the world's love affair with our national flower.

new heights

above right: Rampant Ramblers and slightly tamer Climbers do a superb job of camouflaging utility sheds and other mundane outbuildings. Give vigorous roses room to grow and strong supports.

going wild

right: Selecting a rose that's native to your area enhances its chances of survival. Most of the roses tested by All-America Rose Selections (AARS) are rated for climate.

towering power

left: Large-flowered Climbers and tall-growing Shrubs offer endless possibilities for any landscape. They cover arbors and pergolas quickly. They also provide color and privacy. Take the repeat-flowering examples here: Fragrant yellow 'Lichtkönigin Lucia' (Shrub) grows to 6 feet. Orange-red 'Danse du Feu,' a cluster-flowered Climber with strong fragrance, grows 8 to 12 feet tall and tolerates some shade. The red Shrub 'Hamburger Phoenix' ('Hamburg Rising') reaches 8 to 9 feet and produces large hips (seedpods).

introduction

growing and using roses

Most roses don't deserve their reputation as being demanding plants, although they do require basic care. This book will guide you through the processes of planting, pruning, and feeding your roses as well as training and watering them properly. Discover how to prepare the plants for winter and propagate them, too.

Bringing the beauty and scent of roses indoors is one of the pleasures of growing them. Cut fresh buds and blooms to arrange into bouquets and wreaths; gather fresh petals for culinary use, or dry petals for a simple potpourri.

a few definitions for starters:

Bud eye: a small node on a stem (cane) where stems, leaves, and flower develop.

Bud union: the knobby protrusion on the lower part of the plant where a rose was budded, or grafted, onto a rootstock.

Cane: stem of a rose plant.

Graft: a rose budded onto a rootstock; most modern roses are grafted.

Hybrid: the result of crossing two species or varieties.

Own–root: a rose growing from its own roots.

Remontant: flowering twice or more in a season.

Rootstock: a root chosen for its hardiness, disease resistance, and ability to support a wide range of budded varieties.

Sport: natural mutation in flower color or plant habit. Occasionally sports revert back.

Sucker: a cane growing from below the bud union, from the rootstock.

exquisite scents

right: Gather buds and blossoms, then transform them into a variety of decorative arrangements. Use our recipes to savor their scents with old-fashioned crafts, beauty treatments, and charming edible delicacies.

aromatic shade
above: Climbers
and Ramblers grow
freely up into and
across a pair of trees
to create a fragrant
and shady bower.

prevention pays
left: Stroll daily among
your roses and look
closely at them to
keep ahead of
potential problems.
Take a preventive
approach to pests
and diseases.

the roses

the roses

Just look and you'll find ideal roses for any landscape situation. Because of their myriad growth habits, flower colors, and bloom times, roses make excellent specimens, hedges, groundcovers, container plants, and border companions. The flowers, however, dominate most gardeners' choices. Petal patterns include single (five petals), semidouble (two rows of petals), and double (so packed they hide the flower's center). Bloom shapes vary, too, from blowsy and voluptuous to open and revealing showy stamens. Some form cups; others hold tight points. Some roses bloom repeatedly over the growing season; others produce flowers for one short period (up to six weeks), but in profusion. Explore the two general categories of roses: Heirloom and Modern.

heirloom roses Call them what you will—Old Garden roses or Antique, Heritage, or Heirloom roses—these venerable beauties never lose their appeal. Coming to us through centuries of wild and cultivated growth, these easy-to-grow plants display their survival skills with disease resistance, little need for care, and tolerance of extreme climates. The exquisite beauty of their soft-color flowers parallels their robust fragrance. Most Heirlooms bloom once a year, but some flower off and on from summer into fall. As shrubs, Heirloom roses reach various sizes, making attractive hedge or specimen plants. Choose from Climbers and Ramblers as well as groundcovering varieties.

modern roses Modern hybrids improve on the disease resistance of their older relatives, and most of them produce flowers from late spring to fall. Blooms come in a much wider palette of colors than those of Heirloom roses, including every color except black or a true blue. Modern roses offer a wide range of sizes especially suitable for today's smaller yards and for containers. The newest classes of roses, namely the modern Shrub and Landscape types, often grow wider than tall and make excellent groundcovers as well as low hedges. For years, as roses were bred to be more floriferous and more disease resistant, their flowers tended to be less fragrant. Newer roses, such as the David Austin English roses and the French Romantica roses, in addition to others, have regained that elusive quality as breeders meet gardeners' demands for fragrant flowers showing that ease of care and multiple applications in the landscape cannot replace what first enticed the world to roses.

heirloom roses

alba

As one of the oldest classes of roses, Alba dates back to the Middle Ages when it was cultivated for medicinal use. Although the name means white, Albas bloom in pale pink shades as well. These disease-resistant roses grow well with little attention. Plant them as gracefully arching specimens or as a lush hedge. You'll enjoy their nearly smooth or slightly prickly canes and exceptional blue-gray-green foliage. Give Albas a place in sun or partial shade, in enriched or poor soil, and they will withstand the challenge of less-than-perfect conditions. The plants need only minimal pruning.

Although Albas bloom only once—in early or midsummer—the fragrant flowers are worth the wait.

'Maxima'

'Félicité Parmentier'

'Semi-Plena'

'Madame Plantier'

'Königin von Dänemark'

Clockwise, from top left:

'Maxima'
'The Jacobite Rose'
An ancient, durable rose with double, blush-pink flowers that turn creamy white. It blooms for six weeks; forms orange hips (seedpods) in autumn.

'Félicité Parmentier'
(1834) A 4-foot-tall shrub that's suitable for small gardens. The soft pink flowers exude a delicate, powdery fragrance.

'Madame Plantier'
(1835) A sprawling shrub that reaches 6 feet tall and wide, and features large clusters of small pompon flowers. It thrives in partial shade.

'Königin von Dänemark'
'Queen of Denmark'
(1826) Perfectly shaped, exquisitely scented pink flowers weigh down the 4-foot-long stems, creating a fountain of color.

'Semi-Plena,'
'White Rose of York'
A tough rose that produces large, extremely fragrant white blooms with golden stamens. A first-class shrub that grows best in full sun.

heirloom roses: bourbon

Best known for their heady fragance, Bourbon roses produce large blooms in late spring and sporadically into fall. Found in the 1820s on the Île de Bourbon, east of Madagascar, the original Bourbon rose was a natural hybrid between China and Autumn Damask roses.

Plant Bourbons in a sunny location. Protect tall specimens from strong winds by planting them against a south-facing wall. Encourage blooming through the season by lightly pruning canes after flowers fade. Plants vary from short and compact to upright and spreading. Train taller varieties as climbers or prune them into shrublike shapes.

Although Bourbons are heat-resistant, some develop black spots in areas where the disease prevails.

'Zéphirine Drouhin'

'Madame Isaac Pereire'

'Bourbon Queen'

general characteristics

Overall form: vigorous small to large bushes.
Size: 3 to 15 feet tall, 4 to 5 feet wide.
Bloom time: late spring or early summer and intermittently through the growing season.
Fragrance: rich and varied scents.
Zones: 5–9.

Produces white, pink, deep rose, and variegated flowers, typically in clusters of three.

more great bourbon roses
'Boule de Neige' (milky white)
'Kathleen Harrop' (pale pink)
'Louise Odier' (rose-pink)
'Madame Lauriol de Barny' (silvery pink)
'Reine des Violettes' (lilac-purple)
'Reine Victoria' (rose-pink)
'Souvenir de la Malmaison' (pink)
'Souvenir du Président Lincoln' (rose-red)

'Variegata di Bologna'

'Madame Ernst Calvat'

Clockwise, from top left:
'Zéphirine Drouhin'
(1868) A climbing rose
that grows as a shrub with
pruning. A nearly
thornless plant, it
produces flowers from
early summer into fall. It is
susceptible to black spot
and mildew.

'Madame Isaac Pereire'
(1881) Marvelously
fragrant, classic cabbage-
shape pink blooms appear
in midseason and repeat
in autumn. This upright,
bushy, and spreading rose
is also disease-resistant
and winter-hardy.

'Variegata di Bologna'
(1909) Purple-red stripes
color the creamy white
flowers. After its first, lush
bloom in late spring, it
flowers only sporadically.
The shrub grows to 6 feet;
train the long canes on
a support.

'Madame Ernst Calvat'
(1888) A 6-foot-tall shrub
that grows vigorously. The
lavender-pink blooms
have a heady fragrance.

'Bourbon Queen'
(1834) This repeat
bloomer tolerates shade
and poor soil. Prune it to
a 6-foot shrub or let it
climb to 12 feet on a wall
or arbor.

heirloom roses: centifolia

You see Centifolias in many paintings of the Old Dutch Masters. The lush layers of petals gave rise to the nickname: cabbage rose.

Centifolias date to the 16th century. They have evolved with many species in their parentage. Dutch breeders were largely responsible for developing the class.

The large bushes produce double, strongly fragrant flowers. The heavy blooms nod under their own weight. Centifolias produce a glorious annual show.

The plants require little pruning; deadhead them to keep spent flowers from rotting on the bush. Place them in full sun where air moves freely to minimize disease. Cut out the oldest, weakest canes after the blooming season to encourage new shoots from the plant's base.

'Fantin–Latour'

'Petite de Hollande'

general characteristics

Overall form: large bushes with arching stems.
Size range: 3 to 6 feet tall, 3 to 5 feet wide.
Bloom time: one flush of bloom in late spring or early summer.
Fragrance: splendid, rich scents.
Zones: 5–9.

Large, nodding flowers in shades of pink, mauve, and purple as well as white.

more great centifolia roses

'Blanchefleur' (creamy white)
cabbage rose; *Rosa centifolia* (deep pink)
'Cristata' (pink)
'Robert le Diable' (crimson)
'Shailer's Provence' (light pink)
'Tour de Malakoff' (mauve)
'Village Maid' (off–white striped with pink)

'Rose de Meaux'

'Paul Ricault'

Clockwise, from top left:
'Fantin–Latour'
(1900) Large clusters of fragrant, double flowers grace the garden in midsummer. It tolerates light shade and survives in Zone 4.

'Rose de Meaux'
(1829) An ideal rose for pots, it reaches 18 to 36 inches tall. Bushy and upright, it features tiny pink flowers and diminutive leaves.

'Paul Ricault'
(1845) A strong, upright bush with a heavy spring bloom. The plant produces richly colored, silky flowers in a fountain of fragrant blooms.

'Petite de Hollande'
(early 1800s) A compact bush that grows 3 to 4 feet tall and produces petite 2-inch blooms. A good selection for small gardens and containers.

heirloom roses: china

'Mutabilis'

Cultivated for centuries in China, the China rose *(Rosa chinensis)* came to Europe in 1792 and changed the world of rose breeding more than any other species. The remontancy (repeat flowering) of Chinas set them apart from other roses at the time and has become one of the most desirable qualities of a rose. Their remontancy and heat tolerance have been bred into countless Modern roses.

These twiggy shrubs typically reach 2 to 3 feet tall; some varieties grow to 6 feet or more. Their sweet, fruit-scented blooms continue throughout the summer months.

Although not as hardy as other Heirloom roses, many China roses feature disease resistance and tolerate alkaline and clay soils. They fare well in the heat and humidity of Southern gardens.

'Old Blush'

general characteristics

Overall form: small, compact shrubs; some climbers. Twiggy growth; sparse foliage.
Size range: 2 to 6 feet tall, 3 to 4 feet wide.
Bloom time: late spring to fall.
Fragrance: light to heavy scent.
Zones: 6–9 (with winter protection in Zone 6).

Good for small gardens. Prefer full sun. Dramatically floriferous. Colors range from light pink through crimson; white is unusual.

more great china roses

'Archduke Charles' (red)

'Cramoisi Supérieur' (crimson)

'Ducher' (white)

'Louis Philippe' (red)

'Semperflorens' (deep pink to scarlet)

'Slater's Crimson China' (red)

Clockwise, from top left:

'Mutabilis'
(1800s) The fully open flowers resemble butterflies, hence its other name, the Butterfly Rose. The flowers open yellow and mature to pink, then crimson, with all of these colors displayed on the bush at once. This graceful plant trains easily into a climbing form. Powdery mildew may be a problem in the South.

'Hermosa'
(1840) A slightly fragrant, continual bloomer that features cup-shape buds. The compact, 3-foot-tall plant grows beautifully in a container or as a neat bush in a small garden.

'Old Blush'
'Parson's Pink China'
(1759) One of the original China roses introduced into Europe, it grows as a bush or a climber and has become a classic Old Garden rose. The dainty flowers form small clusters and smell similar to sweet peas. It blooms constantly except during the hottest summer months.

'Hermosa'

heirloom roses: damask

These ancient roses date to Biblical times and consist of two groups. Roses in the first group flower once in early summer. Those in the second group, Autumn Damasks, repeat-flower in late summer or fall.

Brought to Europe by the Crusaders, Damasks became popular not only for their ability to repeat-bloom but also for their rich, deep fragrance. They have been used for centuries to produce attar of roses, a pure essential oil distilled from the flowers for making fine perfumes.

Damasks have shared in the parentage of many subsequent hybrids, in particular, the Portlands.

Plant Damasks in full or partial sun and give them plenty of room to sprawl. Gather their petals for potpourri or other fragrant crafts or cosmetics.

'Madame Hardy'

'Autumn Damask'

general characteristics

Overall form: pointed gray-green leaves on sprawling plants with thorny, arching canes.
Size range: 3 to 5 feet tall, 3 feet wide.
Bloom time: summer; Autumn Damasks repeat bloom in fall.
Fragrance: distinctive and strong.
Zones: 4–9 (with winter protection in Zone 4).

Plant in full or partial sun. Colors range from white and cream to pink and rose.

more great damask roses

'Comte de Chambord' (clear pink)

'Hebe's Lip' (cream edged with red)

'Ispahan' (deep pink)

'La Ville de Bruxelles' (deep pink)

'Leda' (white edged with crimson)

'Petite Lisette' (rosy pink)

'Celsiana'

'Marie Louise'

Clockwise, from top left:
'Madame Hardy' (1832) A strong, lush bush with beautifully double and aromatic creamy white flowers that open flat to expose green centers. This upright plant blooms once.

'Celsiana' (1732) After a single early-summer bloom, the fragrant, soft pink flowers fade as they mature. It features gray-green foliage and tolerates some light shade.

'Marie Louise' (1813) A 4-foot shrub with lush foliage. The large, full blossoms weigh down the cane ends, causing them to arch and touch the ground. Let it sprawl on a fence or low wall.

'Autumn Damask' Until the arrival of the China roses in Europe, this intensely fragrant rose was the only repeat bloomer in Europe. Also known as 'Quatre Saisons' (Four Seasons), it grows into a gracefully spreading bush with ruffled, clear pink blooms and gray-green foliage.

heirloom roses: gallica

The oldest of all garden roses, Gallicas date back thousands of years. Easy to grow, Gallicas tolerate poor soils, wind, and frigid climates but don't fare well in hot, humid areas. They'll grow in sun or partial shade and in dry (but not wet) soil, pleasing you with their disease and pest resistance. Gallicas bloom once in June in a sweetly fragrant and prolific show. Descended from wild roses of southern Europe, they feature nearly thornless stems and dark green foliage.

When grown on their own roots, Gallicas produce suckers (growth from just below the soil line), and easily form dense, natural hedges. The shrubs provide exceptional cut flowers and scarlet-orange hips.

Gallicas figure in the parentage of many Modern roses, especially Portlands.

'Apothecary's Rose'

'Rosa Mundi'

'Duchesse d'Angoulême'

general characteristics

Overall form: both compact and medium-height shrubs that form dense hedges and suit small gardens; taller forms are ideal for trellises.
Size range: 3 to 4 feet tall and wide.
Bloom time: early summer.
Fragrance: light scent.
Zones: 4–8.

Wide range of flower forms. Colors range from pink and crimson to lavender and purple.

more great gallica roses

'Belle Isis' (light pink)

'Cardinal de Richelieu' (mauve-purple)

'Charles de Mills' (crimson fading to red-purple)

'Hippolyte' (magenta-purple)

'Nestor' (lilac-pink)

'Tuscany,' 'Old Velvet' (maroon)

'Tuscany Superb' (crimson-purple)

'Complicata'

'Belle de Crécy'

Clockwise, from top left:
'Apothecary's Rose'
Rosa gallica 'officinalis'
'Red Rose of Lancaster'
This tenacious survivor was brought from Damascus to France by Crusaders in the 13th century. The dried petals retain their fragrance better than those of any other rose.

'Rosa Mundi'
Rosa gallica versicolor
This is the oldest striped rose, said to be named after Fair Rosamund, mistress of King Henry II of England. An excellent rose with bushy growth that makes a fine, 4-foot-tall hedge.

'Complicata'
A shade-tolerant beauty that grows well into trees, using branches for support to reach up to 7 feet. The 5-petaled flowers open to 4 inches across.

'Belle de Crécy'
(1848) This reliable, 4-foot-tall plant has richly fragrant flowers that fade to pale violet in a succession of tints.

'Duchesse d'Angoulême'
(1827) The 3-foot-tall plants feature arching growth with few thorns and light green foliage. In full bloom, the flowers appear to be transparent.

roses | **27**

heirloom roses: hybrid perpetual

Contrary to their name, Hybrid Perpetual's don't bloom constantly. Most flower twice during the growing season. Their large, fragrant blooms make them ideal candidates for cutting.

To prompt increased flowering as well as new growth, bend the long, sturdy cane tips down to touch the ground and secure them in a process known as pegging.

Although they vary in vigor, Hybrid Perpetuals prove hardy in most regions. Grown more for flowers than for appearance in the garden, the slender shrubs need regular watering, abundant fertilization, and afternoon shade.

Immensely popular during the Victorian Age, this complex group of roses represents vast hybridization that focused on developing perfect blooms.

general characteristics

Overall form: vigorous, upright shrubs with strong canes; often lean and lanky.
Size range: 4 to 6 feet tall, 3 to 4 feet wide.
Bloom time: early summer and fall.
Fragrance: most are fragrant.
Zones: 5–9 (with winter protection in Zone 5).

Vary in cold hardiness and disease resistance.
Colors: white, pink to mauve, and red.

more great hybrid perpetuals

'American Beauty' (dark pink)
'Baronne Prévost' (deep rose-pink)
'Gloire de Ducher' (purple-crimson and maroon)
'La Reine' (lilac-pink)
'Paul Neyron' (rose-pink)
'Souvenir du Docteur Jamain' (port wine-violet)

'Ards Rover'

'Frau Karl Druschki'

'Reine des Violettes'

'Baron Girod de l'Ain'

'Mrs John Laing'

Clockwise, from top left:
'Ards Rover'
(1898) A climbing Hybrid Perpetual, it reaches 8 to 12 feet tall and stands up to heat. The flowers repeat sparingly throughout the summer.

'Baron Girod de l'Ain'
(1897) A strong-growing plant that produces clusters of fragrant flowers with ruffled white edges and is prone to disease.

'Mrs. John Laing'
(1887) This reliable, 4-foot shrub with small thorns was one of the most popular roses of its time. It forms gorgeous clusters of three or four blooms.

'Reine des Violettes'
(1860) A beautiful, almost thornless shrub with sweetly scented flowers that fade to violet as they age. It grows easily, even in poor soil.

'Frau Karl Druschki'
(1901) An elegant, long-stemmed beauty with unscented, large white flowers that appear in summer and repeat in fall. It grows to 6 feet and works well at the back of a border. Prune plants to 4 feet, and group three of them for a satisfying effect.

heirloom roses: moss

The original Moss roses were unusual sports or mutations of Centifolia and Damask roses. A mossy growth appears on the sepals at the base of the flowers and stems. Moss roses may have remained little more than curiosities, except that gardeners in Victorian England cherished these charming roses for their distinctive appearance and heady fragrance.

Blooms appear primarily in early summer. If you prune old canes that have finished flowering, new growth produces a wealth of blooms the following summer. Among the thorniest of roses, the plants reflect their varied parentage with a variety of forms: compact, broad, and upright.

For best results, enrich the soil and mulch to keep it moist.

'Crested Moss'

'Henri Martin'

'Alfred de Dalmas'

general characteristics

Overall form: varies from compact to broadly arching and stoutly upright.
Size range: 3 to 4 feet tall and wide.
Bloom time: summer; some repeat.
Fragrance: scented buds, flowers, and stems.
Zones: 4–9.

Susceptible to mildew after flowering. Colors range from white to pink, red, and purple.

more great moss roses

'Duchesse de Verneuil' (pink)
'Little Gem' (pale pink)
Rosa × centifolia 'Muscosa,' 'Common Moss' (deep pink)
'Nuits de Young' (purple-violet-mauve)
'Salet' (bright pink)
'Shailer's White Moss' (white)
'William Lobb' (purple-mauve)

Clockwise, from top left:
'Crested Moss'
'Chapeau de Napoléon'
(1826) This strong and
upright 6-foot-tall bush
features fragrant, double
flowers that bloom once.

'Henri Martin'
'Old Red Moss'
(1863) Blooming once, it
grows 5 to 6 feet tall. This
classic favorite tolerates
some shade. The fragrant
crimson flowers grow
in clusters.

'Blanche Moreau'
(1880) Double, paper-
white flowers contrast
with their brownish moss
and boast intense
fragrance. This slender
plant grows to 6 feet tall.

'Alfred de Dalmas'
'Mousseline'
(1855) A fine, aromatic
Moss rose that reaches
3 feet tall and suits small
gardens beautifully. Its
pink-tinted creamy flowers
appear recurrently
throughout the summer.

'Blanche Moreau'

heirloom roses: noisette

Noisette roses represent the first class of roses born in the United States. They are bred in South Carolina and were further hybridized in France. Their parentage includes China, Musk, and Tea roses. This group of roses is believed to be largely responsible for contributing yellow and orange blooms to many Climbing roses.

Tall, graceful, and everblooming, most Noisettes climb readily and produce drooping clusters of flowers with a distinctive musk scent.

For the most beautiful results, support the rambling plants with a pillar, an arbor, or a pergola; or let them climb on a wall or fence or into a tree.

Noisettes thrive in the mild climate of the South where many old varieties of these roses have been discovered. They're not cold hardy and they often develop black spot and powdery mildew.

'Maréchal Niel'

'Louise D'Arzens'

'Champneys' Pink Cluster'

'Madame Alfred Carrière'

general characteristics

Overall form: large, graceful climbers or shrubs with clusters of small or large flowers.
Size range: 5 to 20 feet tall.
Bloom time: summer to fall.
Fragrance: very heady musk scent on most..
Zones: 7–10.

Excellent for Southern gardens; not cold hardy. Colors range from yellow and white to pink.

more great noisette roses

'Blush Noisette' (pale pink and cream)

'Céline Forestier' (creamy yellow)

'Jeanne d'Arc' (white)

'Lamarque' (white with yellow centers)

'Nastarana' (white touched with pink)

'Rêve d'Or' (yellow)

heirloom roses: portland

This small-distinctive group of roses has proven difficult to trace but appears to be closely related to the Hybrid Perpetuals. The development of these dense, repeat-blooming shrubs began in the 1790s. A handful of varieties remain from their heyday in the mid-1800s.

Portland roses offer fragrant and frequently double blooms on short stems. They feature smooth canes and shiny, light green leaves. The compact and upright roses, mostly between 3 and 5 feet tall, make delightful plants, especially in small gardens. The strong, bushy plants fit nicely in most gardens, however.

The hardiness of Portlands varies. Protect them over winter in cold climates. Provide plants with enriched soil along with plenty of fertilizer and water to keep them healthy and vigorous.

'Jacques Cartier'

'Comte de Chambord'

general characteristics

Overall form: mostly compact, bushy plants; semidouble and double flowers.
Size range: 3 to 5 feet tall, 2 to 3 feet wide.
Bloom time: summer; most repeat into fall.
Fragrance: lovely, sweet scent.
Zones: 4–9 (with winter protection in Zone 4).

Prefer rich soil. Colors range from pink and red to purple.

more great portland roses
'Blanc de Vibert' (white)
'Indigo' (purple)
'Miranda' (pink)
'Portland Rose' (cerise–red)
'Rembrandt' (red with white flecks)
'Rose du Roi' (purple-mottled red)
'Yolande d'Aragon' (bright pink)

'Rose de Rescht'

'Duchess of Portland'

Clockwise, from top left:
'Jacques Cartier'
'Marquise Bocella'
(1868) It produces clusters of 4-inch-wide pink blossoms that have a sweet fragrance. This upright and bushy plant blooms continually during the summer.

'Comte de Chambord'
'Madame Boll'
(1860) This strong, upright bush reaches 4 feet and blooms intermittently after its first flush in early summer. The fragrant, bright pink blooms age to lilac-tinted pink. One of the best Portlands.

'Duchess of Portland'
'The Portland Rose'
(1790) Semidouble, bright red blooms with large petals and yellow stamens appear throughout the growing season. A compact, 3-foot-tall plant, it's suited to small gardens.

'Rose de Rescht'
This neat, shapely bush displays purple-crimson flowers. Repeat blooming and wonderfully fragrant, the plant spreads to only 3 feet. The gray-green foliage is edged with red when young.

As native wild plants from around the world, Species roses make outstanding garden shrubs because of their resilient nature and variety of forms. They usually bloom only once in the season, but they tolerate poor conditions and offer disease resistance. Most also produce large hips (seedpods), which attract and feed birds.

Species roses suit informal, naturalistic garden designs. Place them near the perimeter of your property or at the edge of a wooded area to create a haven where wildlife can find nesting spots, safety, and food.

Plant and forget Species roses, if you want, until they put on their late spring flower show. Prune the plants only to keep them in bounds and to remove damaged or dead canes.

Most modern roses have descended from a handful of Species roses.

Rosa rugosa 'Hansa'

Rosa foetida 'Harison's Yellow'

Rosa glauca

general characteristics

Overall form: large, open, bristly shrubs with small single or semidouble flowers.
Size range: 4 to 20 feet, depending on species.
Bloom time: spring to early summer; once.
Fragrance: some have scent.
Zones: depends on species; generally hardy.

Easy to grow; some can be invasive. Colors include red, pink, yellow, and white.

more great species roses

Rosa banksiae lutea 'Lady Banks' Rose (yellow)
Rosa canina 'Dog Rose' (light pink)
Rosa eglanteria 'Sweetbriar' (pink)
Rosa laevigata 'Cherokee Rose' (white)
Rosa nutkana 'Nootka Rose' (red to purple–pink)
Rosa rugosa 'Alba' (white)
Rosa. spinosissima 'Scotchbriar' (cream)
Rosa. tomentosa 'Downy Rose' (pink)

Rosa multiflora 'Carnea'

Rosa roxburghii 'Chestnut Rose'

Clockwise, from top left:

R. rugosa 'Hansa'
(1905) This double-flowered Rugosa hybrid with prickly stems and crinkled leaves (rugosa means wrinkled) is easy to grow. It's hardy in Zones 3–8 and grows 7 feet tall and wide.

R. foetida var. persiana 'Harison's Yellow'
(1830) The 'Yellow Rose of Texas' produces semidouble flowers in late spring; it grows 5 to 8 feet tall and 4 feet wide. Native to Asia and tough as nails, it spread across North America with the pioneers. It's hardy in Zones 6–9.

R. multiflora 'Carnea'
(1804) Part of Empress Josephine's gardens at Malmaison, it blooms in spring in Zones 5–9.

R. roxburghii 'Chestnut Rose'
(pre-1800s) Hardy in Zones 5–9, this disease-resistant beauty easily forms a living fence but has a reputation for outgrowing its welcome.

R. glauca; R. rubrifolia
(pre-1830) Coppery gray foliage and stems that arch more than 14 feet. This rose is hardy in Zones 4–9.

Varieties of the Tea rose (*Rosa × odorata*) came to Europe from China in the early 1800s. The class was a centuries-old hybrid between *R. gigantea* and *R. chinensis*. The former gave the Tea its fragrance, the latter its everblooming trait. Tea roses are among the parents of the first Hybrid Tea roses.

Tea roses often grow as climbers, producing large, fragrant flowers and few thorns. They typically feature woody canes colored from plum to bronze. Teas are hardy only in frost-free areas of California and the South. Enjoy the exceptional cut flowers of Tea roses as well as their minimal need for pruning. Cut only old or dead canes and trim off spent blooms. Plant Tea roses in well-drained, fertile soil in a sunny and protected location.

general characteristics

Overall form: climbers or small bushes, usually with few thorns.
Size range: 3 to 10 feet.
Bloom time: all season.
Fragrance: classic Tea rose scent.
Zones: 7–10.

Colors range from buff and yellow to various shades of pink.

more great tea roses

'Gloire de Dijon' (buff-apricot)

'Lady Hillingdon' (apricot-copper)

'Mrs. B.R. Cant' (pink tipped)

'Mrs. Dudley Cross' (pale yellow–pink blend)

'Sombreuil' (creamy white)

'Madame Bérard'

'Monsieur Tillier'

'Madame Antoine Rébé'

Clockwise, from top left:
'Madame Bérard'
(1870) A climbing Tea
whose parentage includes
'Gloire de Dijon,' it
reaches 12 to 15 feet tall
on a trellis or wall. It
features lush blooms with
a fruity fragrance and
disease resistance.

'Madame Antoine
Rébé'
(1900) The dense foliage
and slender growing habit
of this Tea rose are
reminiscent of early China
roses. The blooms have a
slight fragrance. It grows
to about 4 feet tall. A
disease-resistant plant.

'Monsieur Tillier'
(1891) This outstanding
rebloomer produces
fragrant, purplish carmine
flowers on a compact,
4-foot-tall shrub.

modern roses
climbers

Most Climbing roses are either large-flowering or cluster-flowering variations or mutations of bush-type roses. These vigorous plants produce canes that reach 6 to 20 feet tall. Depending on the variety, they bloom once a year, repeatedly, or throughout the growing season.

Climbers make outstanding accents, clambering over a trellis, an arbor, a pergola, a wall, or a fence. Unlike tendrils on vines, rose thorns don't help them climb and cling to a support. During a plant's first few summers in the garden, train it to climb by loosely tying its canes to a support. Gently guide canes in a horizontal direction to encourage more bloom.

'Dortmund'

Rosa banksiae var. banksiae

'Blaze'

'New Dawn'

Fortune's Double Yellow

Clockwise, from top left:

'Dortmund'
(1955) Hardy to Zone 4, this disease-resistant Climber grows 7 to 10 feet tall, with blooms in summer and orange hips in fall. It will rebloom if you remove the spent flowers instead of letting the plant produce hips.

Rosa banksiae var. banksiae
(1796) Fragrant flowers appear in spring on an almost thornless plant. It grows quickly to more than 25 feet. Other varieties of the banksiae species include single-flowered *normalis* (white) and *lutea* (yellow).

'New Dawn'
(1930) One of the best Climbers around, this disease-resistant beauty grows 10 to 18 feet tall and produces fragrant flowers all season.

'Fortune's Double Yellow'
(1845) Delicate-looking and graceful (but thorny), this Climber blooms once in spring and reaches 6 to 10 feet tall.

'Blaze'
(1932) Fast-growing and disease-resistant, this plant climbs to 12 feet and blooms all summer.

modern roses: floribunda

Exceptional as landscape and bedding roses, Floribundas require little care and bloom profusely all season. Their compact growth habit makes them ideal for a mass display of color in a hedge or edging, depending on the size of the garden. They make perfect partners planted in front of tall, leggy roses, such as Grandifloras. Pot Floribundas to create spots of concentrated, lasting color.

The flowers, slightly smaller than those of Hybrid Teas, occur in clusters and are single, semidouble, or double. They bloom all summer.

Floribundas are more disease-resistant and hardier than Hybrid Teas. They need winter protection in cold climates.

'Hannah Gordon'

'French Lace'

'Iceberg'

general characteristics

Overall form: mostly upright-growing shrubs that produce clusters of flowers.
Size: 2 to 4 feet tall and wide.
Bloom time: all season.
Fragrance: many have fragrance.
Zones: 4–9.

Colors range from white and pink to yellow, red, and striped or bicolors.

more great floribunda roses

'Allgold' (yellow)

'Apricot Nectar' (soft apricot)

'China Doll' (pink)

'Europeana' (deep red)

'Grüss an Aachen' (pink)

'Johann Strauss' (pale pink)

'Lilli Marleen' (red)

'Marmalade Skies' (tangerine)

'Nearly Wild' (rosy pink)

'Sexy Rexy' (pink)

'Sunsprite' (deep yellow)

Clockwise, from top left:
'Hannah Gordon'
(1983) An admirable rose for beds and borders that reaches medium height. It offers dark bronze-green foliage and white blooms edged with cherry pink.

'French Lace'
(1980) Spice-scented blooms form in clusters and appear throughout the summer. Hardy to Zone 4, it grows up to 3 feet tall and offers disease resistance.

'Betty Prior'
(1935) Lightly scented, dogwoodlike flowers become more reddish in cool weather. The upright, vigorous, 5-foot-tall bush is disease-resistant and excellent for mass plantings.

'Iceberg'
(1958) Valued as one of the finest white roses around, this superior landscape bush produces fragrant flowers all summer on a vigorous plant. Almost thornless, it's ideal for containers, too.

'Betty Prior'

modern roses: grandiflora

Tall and strong, Grandifloras exhibit the best traits of their parents: the classic flower form of Hybrid Tea and the hardiness, continuous flowering, and clustered blooms of Floribunda. The class was created in the United States to accommodate 'Queen Elizabeth,' considered the prototype of the perfect Grandiflora when it was introduced in 1954.

These are excellent landscape roses that grow to 6 feet tall; one long stem erupts in an entire bouquet of large roses. Now widely termed cluster-flowered roses, they're useful for cut flowers as well as for background color in the garden. The vigorous shrubs are popular as hedges and screens. They are typically disease resistant and cold hardy.

'Caribbean'

'Gold Medal'

'Octoberfest'

'Fame!'

'Tournament of Roses'

general characteristics

Overall form: tall plants with clusters of
flowers on a long stem.
Size: 4 to 6 feet tall.
Bloom time: continuous all summer.
Fragrance: some are scented.
Zones: 5–9.

Generally hardy. Colors include all rose colors.
Good for screening and for cut flowers.

more great grandiflora roses

'Aquarius' (light pink)

'Glowing Peace' (amber-pink blend)

'Love' (red with white reverse)

'Queen Elizabeth' (pink)

'Sheer Bliss' (creamy white flushed with pink)

'Shreveport' (orange blend)

'Sonia' (coral-pink)

modern roses: hybrid tea

The result of crossing Tea roses with Hybrid Perpetuals in the mid-1800s, the first Hybrid Teas represented their parents' best traits, including elegance, vigor, and repeat blooming, which ensured their popularity from the beginning.

When they first appeared, Hybrid Teas had large, fragrant blooms and a weakness for disease. In subsequent decades, breeders sought to bring disease resistance and cold hardiness to the shrubs. The hybridizers succeeded to some extent, but many of the roses they developed lost the fragrance of their ancestors. Today's plant breeders keep the desirability of scent at the forefront of their efforts to attain the perfect rose.

Elegant buds and exquisite blooms make them the most widely grown roses.

'Honor'

'Peace'

'Brandy'

general characteristics

Overall form: upright plants; flowers on long, single stems.
Size: 3 to 5 feet tall, 3 to 4 feet wide.
Bloom time: off and on all summer.
Fragrance: many are scented.
Zones: 4–9 (with winter protection in Zone 4).

Flowers in all colors except blue; bicolors and blends. Need ample water, fertilizer.

more great hybrid teas

'Chrysler Imperial' (red)

'First Prize' (pink)

'Fragrant Cloud' (coral-orange)

'Garden Party' (creamy white)

'Just Joey' (coppery apricot)

'Mister Lincoln' (deep red)

'Perfume Delight' (pink)

'Pristine' (pink-edged white)

'Touch of Class' (coral-pink, orange, and cream)

'Dainty Bess'

'Double Delight'

Clockwise, from top left:
'Honor'
(1980) Favored for cutting, this prolific, vigorous plant produces exceptional long-stemmed blooms.

'Peace'
(1945) Universally recognized as one of the finest Hybrid Teas, this All-America Rose Selection (AARS) winner is a vigorous, disease-resistant plant with glorious, long-lasting blooms.

'Dainty Bess'
(1925) Unusual for a Hybrid Tea, the bush produces clusters of lightly fragrant, single-petal flowers throughout the summer. This sturdy, elegant plant belies its name.

'Double Delight'
(1977) The bicolor blooms with their delightful, spicy fragrance make this AARS winner ideal for cutting. The medium-height, bushy plant stands out in the garden.

'Brandy'
(1982) This AARS winner combines glossy, disease-resistant foliage with burnt orange buds that open to exquisite golden apricot blooms.

modern roses: miniature

Scarcely known before the 1930s, Miniatures now foster widespread popularity for their petite charms. As dwarf plants, with flowers and foliage in proportion to their size, Miniature roses are available in a wide assortment of colors, flower forms, and growth habits. Some climb to 6 feet tall; others sprawl to 2 feet wide. Some hybrids range from 6 to 18 inches tall.

Ideal for pots, hanging baskets, and windowsills, Miniatures also make excellent edging plants and are just the right touch for a small space. Surprisingly winter-hardy, they are profuse bloomers that require little care. Gather handfuls of Miniature blooms for a vase and enjoy them indoors, too.

'Black Jade'

'Yellow Doll'

'Marriotta'

Clockwise, from top left:
'Black Jade'
(1985) The buds of this velvety red rose are so dark they appear almost black. It grows between 18 and 24 inches tall.

'Marriotta'
(1989) This vigorous plant grows 24 to 36 inches tall and produces delightful flowers in clusters.

'Baby Grand'
(1994) A compact, bushy 12- to 16-inch-tall beauty with bright green leaves. It plays a rhapsody in the garden with apple-scented, perfect pink flowers.

'Gourmet Popcorn'
(1986) This disease-resistant repeat bloomer grows 15 to 24 inches tall. Large clusters of fragrant blooms cascade over the dark green foliage.

'Yellow Doll'
(1962) Long popular, this compact, bushy plant offers disease resistance and winter hardiness. The Hybrid Tea-like blooms carry a light scent.

'Gourmet Popcorn'

'Baby Grand'

modern roses: polyantha

Perfect for beds and low hedges, Polyanthas typically grow knee-high in compact forms that produce small, clustered flowers constantly. Horticulturists crossed Polyanthas with Hybrid Teas giving rise to Floribundas (including some with fragrance). Polyanthas' general hardiness, durability, and landscape utility make up for the lack of fragrance in some varieties.

Plant Polyanthas as a groundcover, an edging along a border, or a foundation shrub. Smaller varieties thrive in containers. Train taller ones, such as climbing sports, up trellises, or let them wend their way through shrubs or perennial borders.

In late winter, prune Polyanthas to remove dead wood and maintain their shape. Snip off spent blooms to keep plants flowering freely.

'Marie Pavié'

'The Fairy'

'Cécile Brünner'

general characteristics

Overall form: mostly compact, rounded plants with clusters of small (1-inch) flowers.
Size: 18 inches to 3 feet tall.
Bloom time: most repeat-bloom all season.
Fragrance: some have light fragrance.
Zones: 4–10.

Withstand heat better than most roses. Colors include pinks, reds, orange, yellow, and white.

more great polyantha roses
'Ballerina' (pink)
'Climbing Cécile Brünner' (pink)
'Happy' (red)
'La Marne' (pink)
'Mignonette' (rosy pink)
'Perle d'Or' (salmon-pink)
'Red Fairy' (cherry-red)
'Violette' (purple-edged violet)

'Margo Koster'

'China Doll'

Clockwise, from top left:

'Marie Pavié'
(1888) Classic pointed buds unfurl into pale, double blooms that boast a delicate fragrance. This thornless plant is hardy to Zone 4 and grows 2 to 4 feet tall.

'The Fairy'
(1932) Perhaps one of the best-known roses for its easy care and delightful presence, this Polyantha produces an abundance of tiny pink flowers from midsummer into fall. It's hardy to Zone 4.

'Margo Koster'
(1931) This tough, compact bush grows 1½ to 3 feet tall and wide. Slightly fragrant blooms repeat into fall.

'China Doll'
(1946) Easy to grow and disease-resistant, the nearly thornless plants reach 1½ feet tall and nearly 3 feet wide. The lightly fragrant flowers almost conceal foliage.

'Cécile Brünner'
'Mlle. Cécile Brünner'
(1881) Called 'The Sweetheart Rose' in generations past, the perfect 1-inch blooms appear from spring to fall and offer a light fragrance.

modern roses: rambler

If left to their inherent devices, graceful Ramblers spread freely in all directions. Give them the sturdy support of a fence, a wall, or a tree, and they'll typically produce a blanket of flowers that will cover their support with a glorious show of color. Gently bend the pliable canes of young plants to train them onto a support, then tie them loosely to it.

Ramblers produce large clusters of small flowers on 1-year-old canes. After flowering, cutting out old canes at the plant's base encourages new canes to form that will produce a wealth of blooms the following summer. Ramblers need minimal pruning, however, so snip with restraint. Remember, part of the beauty of Ramblers is their informal shape.

'May Queen'

'Apple Blossom'

general characteristics

Overall form: vigorous, sprawling, long canes.
Size: 10 to 20 feet tall or more.
Bloom time: bloom once between late spring and midsummer.
Fragrance: many are fragrant.
Zones: 5–9.

Colors include shades of pink, red, yellow, and white. Need sturdy supports.

more great rambler roses

'Albéric Barbier' (pale yellow)

'Albertine' (copper-pink)

'Dr. W. Van Fleet' (pink)

'Dorothy Perkins' (light pink)

'Félicité et Perpétue' (white)

'Léontine Gervais' (copper-pink)

'Paul's Himalayan Musk' (creamy pink)

'Veilchenblau' (purple)

'Gardenia'

'American Pillar'

'Tausendschön'

Clockwise, from top left:
'May Queen'
(1898) A good candidate to grow up into a tree, it produces lovely semidouble, fragrant flowers that open flat. This Rambler blooms once lushly, followed by a few later blooms. It grows 15 to 20 feet tall.

'Apple Blossom'
(1932) Aptly named, it bears apple blossom pink blooms once in spring. Flowers are lightly fragrant. It grows up to 10 feet tall.

'American Pillar'
(1902) Very popular after its introduction, but susceptible to mildew. It produces large clusters of lightly fragrant flowers in midsummer and grows 12 to 20 feet tall.

'Tausendschön'
'Thousand Beauties'
(1906) Once-blooming, it produces a multitude of large flowers and grows about 8 feet tall.

'Gardenia'
(1899) Vigorous, pliable canes train easily and reach 15 to 20 feet tall. The flowers bear a light apple fragrance.

modern roses: shrub

Shrub roses take various forms, from tidy bushes with small clusters of flowers to tall, arching plants or sprawling bushes ideal for hedges. Some bloom once; others bloom repeatedly. Many Shrub roses grow on their own roots instead of being grafted, so their canes grow back if they're killed by winter cold.

Some of the hardiest Shrub roses include Griffith Buck roses, such as 'Carefree Beauty,' developed at Iowa State University; Canadian hybrids, such as the Morden Series, Explorer Series, and Parkland Series; and Meidiland roses, bred by the French House of Meilland. David Austin English Roses, bred by crossing Old roses with Modern repeat-bloomers, imitate Heirloom roses with their blowsy flower forms and lush fragrance.

'Sparrieshoop'

'Fair Bianca'

'Graham Thomas'

'Carefree Wonder'

'Leander'

'Scarlet Meidiland'

Clockwise, from top left:

'Sparrieshoop'
(1953) Varying in shape from shrub to climber, it produces long-lasting, fragrant flowers all summer.

'Fair Bianca'
(1983) This 4-foot-tall David Austin English rose offers strong fragrance and disease resistance.

'Leander'
(1983) This David Austin English rose has fruit-scented flowers and mahogony-colored canes. A strong, upright plant, it grows 4 to 5 feet tall.

'Scarlet Meidiland'
(1987) The disease-resistant, glossy dark green foliage of this hardy Shrub reinforces its stellar reputation.

'Carefree Wonder'
(1990) Disease-resistant, it blooms profusely all summer, reaching 4 feet tall and 3 feet wide.

'Graham Thomas'
(1983) A favorite David Austin English rose, it bears gorgeous large, fragrant blooms. Train as a bush (3 feet tall) or a climber (to 10 feet).

general characteristics

Overall form: compact or sprawling. Single or double flowers.
Size: 2½ to 5 feet tall or more.
Bloom time: most, not all, repeat-bloom.
Fragrance: many are fragrant.
Zones: 3–10 (varies among cultivars).

Flower colors include all the usual shades.
Disease-resistant. Need minimal maintenance.

more great shrub roses

'Alba Meidiland' (white)

'Alchymist' (apricot yellow)

'All That Jazz' (red-salmon)

'Bonica' (pink)

'Carefree Delight' (pink blend)

'Flower Carpet' (red; pink; or white)

'Gertrude Jekyll' (pink)

'Golden Wings' (yellow)

'Henry Kelsey' (red)

'Heritage' (pink)

'Knock Out' (red)

'Mary Rose' (rose-pink)

modern roses:
all-america rose selections

A group of rose breeders and producers formed All-America Rose Selections (AARS) in 1938 to encourage rose research and promotion. The nonprofit group conducts two-year trials and evaluations to help improve the vitality of roses for home gardens in all climates in the country.

Judges rate roses submitted for trial on the basis of many traits, including bud and flower form, vigor, growth habit, hardiness, disease resistance, foliage characteristics, and fragrance. AARS awards go to roses with the highest marks.

Many of the best-known roses grown in gardens today include AARS winners such as 'Peace,' 'Mister Lincoln,' 'Tropicana,' and 'French Lace.'

'Shining Hour'

'Pride 'n' Joy'

'Class Act'

Clockwise, from above:
'Shining Hour'
(1991) A Grandiflora that grows up to 4 feet tall and bears large (4-inch) blooms with a light fragrance.

'Pride 'n' Joy'
(1992) A Miniature with blooms that have the elegance of a full-sized Hybrid Tea. Compact, it grows up to 3 feet tall.

'Class Act'
(1989) A disease-resistant and vigorous Floribunda with an upright habit, it reaches 4 to 5 feet tall and produces blooms with a light fragrance.

'Zéphirine Drouhin'

'Charles de Mills'

Rose thorns represent the painful, even wicked side of growing the otherwise splendid plants. Sharp, piercing thorns injure you if you're not careful. Eliminate the risk by growing thornless varieties that bear few, if any, thorns.

Some of these thornless roses are truly smooth-caned; others have blunted or sparsely scattered prickles on their canes: Choose from 'Belle de Crécy' (Gallica), 'Chloris' (Alba), 'Eugénie Guinoisseau' (Moss), 'Heritage' (Shrub), 'Hippolyte' (Gallica), 'Marie Pavié' (Polyantha), 'Nevada' (Shrub), 'Pacific Serenade' (Miniature), 'Prince Charles' (Bourbon), 'Reine de Violettes' (Hybrid Perpetual), 'Rosa Mundi' (Gallica), and 'Sally Holmes' (Shrub).

Clockwise, from above: 'Zéphirine Drouhin' (1868) A Bourbon rose that grows as a large shrub or a climber and bears lovely, fragrant flowers in late spring or early summer. The winter-hardy plant reaches 8 to 12 feet tall.

'Charles de Mills' (pre-1746) A popular Gallica that produces spectacularly large, red-purple flowers once during summer. The vigorous bush grows 4 to 5 feet tall.

the basics

the basics

will respond with exuberant growth and armloads of blossoms. Planting, pruning, fertilizing, and mulching keep you busy in spring. Then comes the first beautiful flush of colorful flowers, along with time to pause and enjoy them. More fertilizing and pest patrol occupy the summer months. Cut and share your roses, especially if you grow repeat-bloomers. Keep an eye out for potential problems with pests or diseases. Check your plants each day and catch a problem before it becomes insurmountable. The end of the growing season brings rose hips (for you and the birds to savor) as well as winter preparation. **climate control** Climate affects roses in ways you often cannot control. You can, however, temper its effects with your choice of plants and their location in the garden. Some roses, such as Albas and Gallicas, take the cold of Zone 4 winters in stride. Other roses, particularly Rugosas, withstand the wind and salt spray of a seaside locale.

Frigid winters take their toll on some grafted roses. A proper planting method, appropriately timed pruning, and adequate winter protection help plants survive and thrive in cold conditions. If you live in an extreme climate, choose Heirloom roses with tough dispositions and hardiness, proven through generations of survival.

In any climate, take advantage of the sun and shade your site provides. Plant roses in fertile soil to give them a good start, and enrich it regularly to keep them growing strong and healthy. Provide adequate water and regular attention. Then, stand back and savor your success.

The time you spend taking care of your roses becomes a pleasure if you remember that planning and prevention are the keys to having healthy plants and gorgeous flowers. Set up a schedule that leaves you free to stop and smell the roses you grow.

easy does it Cast away the notion that you must constantly spray and otherwise tend your plants to encourage them to produce perfect leaves, buds, and blooms. Start with rich soil and a generous planting hole, and your roses

site & soil

first things first

Get your roses off to the best start possible by giving them a location that serves them, rather than one that suits your idea of a garden design. For best results choose a site that receives at least six hours of sun daily.

Also, select a place with good drainage. Roses need generous amounts of water, but their roots fare poorly in soil that drains too slowly. If you have heavy or clay soil that drains poorly, elevate the roses by planting them in raised beds.

Plant roses away from the canopy of trees and other shrubs, where roots must compete for nutrients.

microclimates work

right: If you plan to grow roses in adverse conditions, such as those in a seaside garden, the desert, or the deep South, site the garden where a building, a hedge, or a backdrop of trees will shelter it from wind and midday sun.

1

planting sense When preparing a planting hole, mix four to six shovelfuls of compost and rotted manure with the backfill to enrich the soil. Loosen soil in the bottom and sides of the planting hole to give roots plenty of growing room. Improve drainage by working a shovelful of powdered gypsum into the bottom of the planting hole.

Roses tolerate a wide range of soils, but they prefer it to be slightly acidic (pH 6.5). A soil test identifies the soil pH level and should be done before planting. If your soil is too acidic, sprinkle a handful of ground limestone around a plant and scratch it into the top 6 inches of soil. If the soil is too alkaline, work in handfuls of ground sulfur.

2

soil helpers Roses grow best in fertile, enriched soil. Any soil merits improvement. Use organic amendments at planting time and seasonally to build up the soil and increase its fertility. Do a soil test before amending your soil to determine if it needs any particular nutrients. Roses require the same basic nutrients as other plants: nitrogen, phosphorous, and potassium, represented as N–P–K on packages of some organic soil amendments and other fertilizers. Roses also need the minerals found in balanced fertilizers or rose food and the microbes available in compost.

Combine organic amendments and apply them a shovelful at a time; no particular ratios are necessary. Use various organic amendments for their specific benefits. For instance, boost nitrogen levels (and promote healthy leaf and stem growth) by adding compost, rotted manure, alfalfa meal, or cottonseed meal.

2

planting

off to a good start

Whether you plant bare-root or container-grown roses that grow on their own roots or on grafted rootstock, dig an ample planting hole. Ideally, plant bare-root roses during early spring in cold climates, during late winter in Zones 7 to 10.

Plant bare-root roses as soon as you get them. If you need to hold off planting for a day, keep the roses in a bucket of water overnight. For a longer duration lay them at a 45-degree angle in a shallow, shaded trench, keeping the roots covered with soil until permanent planting time. Water thoroughly.

adaptable plants

right: Plant container-grown roses from spring through early summer or in early fall. Remove plants from nursery pots or boxes, loosen the soil around the roots, and gently straighten any roots that encircle the sides and bottom of the root ball.

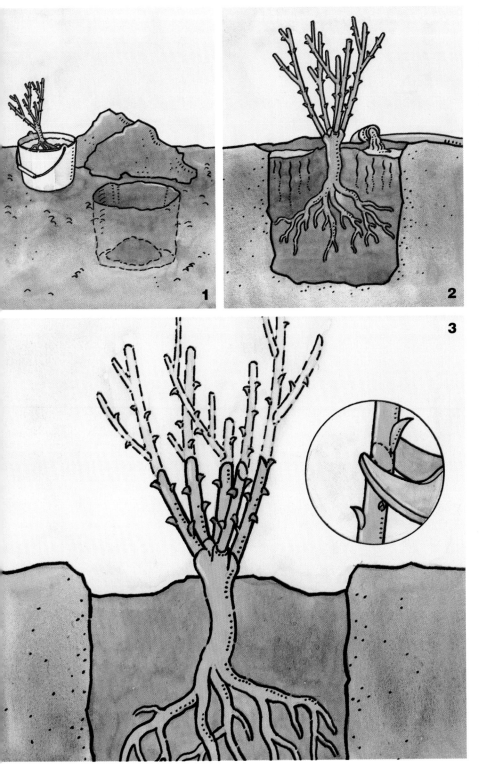

prepare and plant `1` Take a bare-root rose out of the packaging in which it came. Prune off broken canes, and soak the roots in a bucket of water for at least an hour (overnight, at most) to rehydrate them. Add a splash of B vitamins (available at garden centers) to the water to help the plant overcome transplant shock.

Dig a generous planting hole, 12 to 18 inches deep and 2 feet wide, to give the roots growing room. Center a low mound of soil in the bottom of the hole. Prune off any cracked or broken roots; bend or trim roots minimally to fit the hole without breaking them. Position the roots on top of the mounded soil, keeping the bud union (the knobby area where roots join canes on grafted roses) 1 to 2 inches above ground level in mild-winter areas; 1 to 2 inches below soil level in cold-winter areas.

fill and water `2` Backfill the hole halfway with enriched soil. Slowly water the planting, using the B vitamin-enriched water in which the roots soaked earlier. Let the water saturate the soil. Finish filling the planting hole. Water again, using a hose.

Build a shallow moat of soil around the perimeter of the planting hole to collect and channel water to the roots. Moats are unnecessary in a rainy region such as the Pacific Northwest.

prune `3` After planting, cut off all but three to five healthy canes. Prune at an outward-facing, 45-degree angle just above a bud to promote new growth. Aim for an open center that promotes air circulation. Prune all canes to about the same length.

feeding, mulching, & watering

1   **feeding roses** Fertilize roses in spring as leaf buds begin to open. Feed again two to three weeks after the first flush of blooms fades. Fertilize repeat-bloomers once a month thereafter. In cold-winter areas, stop feeding two months before the average first hard frost in fall.

Either water plants with liquid fertilizer or sprinkle granular fertilizer around each plant and scratch it into the soil with a cultivator.

Apply superphosphate, fish emulsion, or fish meal to boost blooming. Many rose growers swear by Epsom salts as a source of magnesium, which promotes healthy growth. Sprinkle ½ cup around the base of each plant in spring and again in midsummer; gently work it into the soil. Other gardeners tuck banana peels into the soil to add potassium, aiming to improve overall plant vigor and strong canes.

2   **mulching** Spread a 3-inch layer of mulch on the soil between plants (away from stems) to help it retain moisture and prevent weed growth. Apply an organic mulch, such as compost, rotted manure, chopped leaves or bark, and alfalfa meal or pellets. Mulch breaks down gradually and adds nutrients to the soil. Replace it seasonally as necessary.

3   **grass mulch** Instead of bagging grass clippings, leaving them on the lawn, or adding them to the compost pile, spread them as a 2-inch-deep mulch on rose beds. But let the clippings dry for a few days before using them. Fresh grass clippings tend to mat when wet, forming an impenetrable covering that prevents soil from absorbing rain.

watering Notoriously thirsty plants, roses need regular watering if rain doesn't come. Water new plantings weekly between rains throughout their first and second summers. Water to a depth of 6 inches; use a trowel to check the saturation level. Before and after fertilizing, water plants to help them absorb nutrients.

In order to survive a drought or water restrictions, most roses go semidormant, producing little new growth or flowers. Hold off on fertilizer if you cannot water.

compost tea Compost tea acts as a mild foliar fertilizer (sprayed on leaves) that also helps prevent powdery mildew and black spot. Steep 1 to 2 cups of compost in 1 gallon of water for several hours; stir well to dissolve. Strain and spray on roses. To eliminate straining, put compost in the legs of an old pair of pantyhose and tie it closed before soaking it in the water.

watering wisdom

The best way to water roses employs a drip irrigation system or soaker hose. With these methods, water goes directly to plant roots, minimizing evaporation and water loss. Set your watering system on a timer to ease the process. Place drip heads in potted roses to water them easily, too.

Avoid watering from overhead with a handheld hose or a sprinkler. Wet foliage fosters disease. Instead, use a hose set on a slow trickle to water only at the base of plants. Or bury a soaker hose under mulch in garden beds for efficient watering.

pruning

the kindest cuts

Pruning intimidates some gardeners. When you understand the reasons for making the cuts, pruning becomes less daunting. Here are the reasons to prune.

Health: The dead or damaged canes of any rose should be cut back to green wood in late winter or early spring, before the plant resumes growth. Remove diseased canes when you notice them. Improve air circulation by removing canes that grow into the center of the plant.

Appearance: Bushy Modern roses need help to maintain their compact, open form. Heirloom roses require less pruning because their lax, twiggy look is part of their charm. Deadheading, or cutting off spent flowers, encourages plants to rebloom.

Control: Some roses grow with wild abandon. Keep them within bounds by pruning their tips or entire canes anytime.

1

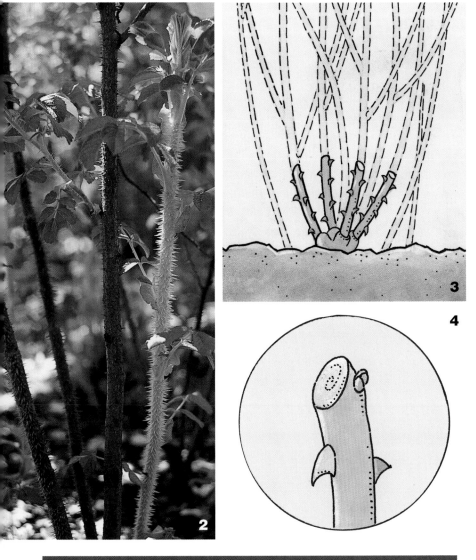

a little pruning Every time you cut
a rose bloom to bring it indoors, you prune
the plant. This is mild, compared to pruning
at the beginning of the season. Roses grow
from the point where they are cut, so
consider the overall shape of the plant as
you snip.

1

healthy cuts Healthy canes appear
green or reddish. Old and dying canes turn
brown. Prune out diseased, weak, broken, or
dead canes whenever you see them. Cut
them back to green wood or close to the
bud union (a swelling at the base of the
plant where the canes join the roots).

2

overall look When pruning roses,
cut out canes that cross, saving the better of
the two. On Modern or grafted roses, prune
away suckers, or canes that arise from the
rootstock, rather than from the plant budded
or grafted onto the rootstock. Aim for a
vase–shape bush with an open center. Prune
to keep the plant symmetrical and balanced.
Arching and climbing roses require little
pruning, in general. Train them to fulfill their
purpose, whether growing on a fence, an
arbor, or a pillar, by pruning after they
bloom. Remove their old and weak canes.

3

proper cut Cut canes at a 45–degree
angle just above a leaf bud (swelling on
the cane). Slant the cut away from the
bud, to encourage growth outward. Clean
pruners after every use to prevent the
spread of disease. Keep pruners sharp to
make clean cuts.

4

pruning roses

rose type	when to prune	region
once–blooming	after blooming, in summer	all regions
repeat–blooming	lightly after blooming	all regions
modern miniature	January to early March late winter, early spring	zones 8–10 zones 4–7
species, heirloom, & shrub	late winter, early spring, lightly after blooming	all regions

propagating cuttings

1 select Heirloom roses, especially, root readily using this method just after they finish blooming. Choose a 1- to 2-foot-long cane; cut off spent flowers. Cut the cane just below a bud eye (node on the cane) in 6-inch pieces at a 45-degree angle. Remove all but the uppermost leaves on each cutting.

2 prepare Dip the bottom of the cutting in a rooting hormone powder. Insert the cutting into a 3-inch peat pot filled with seed-starting mix (a soilless medium), ensuring that at least two bud eyes are buried. Firm the mix around the cutting.

3 plant Place the pot in a plastic bag to help keep the soil moist, and set it in a shady place. In 14 to 20 days, you'll see roots poking out of the pot's bottom. Plant the new rose in the ground, or transplant to a 6-inch pot, then move it to the garden in early fall.

4 protect After planting, protect the rose from the elements for a few days by covering it with a clear glass jar; prop up the jar to let in air. Water regularly until the plant is well-established.

willow wisdom

Rooting hormone powder (available at garden centers) stimulates root development. Also try willow water, an alternative touted by rosarians. Place chopped willow twigs in a jar, cover them with water, and let stand overnight. Soak rose cuttings in willow water for several hours (or overnight) before planting them in pots of soilless mix to root. Saturate the soilless mix with willow water.

prepare In summer, open several buds 1
on your chosen mother plant. Use tweezers to
remove the petals and some anthers, which
stand around the edge of the flower's center
and store pollen. Let buds rest for a day until
the stigmas (on top of the pistils in the flower's
center) looks shiny and wet, which means the
flower is ready for pollination.

pollinate Remove an open flower 2
from the plant selected as the father and
pluck off the petals. Rub the father flower
across the mother bud to distribute pollen.
   Leave the pollinated bud on the mother
plant. Tag it with the name of the parent
plants. Now wait. If the cross-pollination
succeeds, the ovary at the base of the pistils
begins to swell in about three weeks and
develop into a seedpod (rose hip). Let the
seedpod mature on the plant until it turns
dark after a frost. Then cut the pod from the
plant, slit it open, and remove the seeds.
Place the seeds in a plastic bag that's filled
with moist sphagnum moss. Label the bag
and store it in the refrigerator over winter.

sow In early spring, sow the seeds in 3
4-inch pots filled with soilless seed-starting
mix. Set the pots on a sunny windowsill;
keep the mix moist. The seeds should
germinate within four weeks.

move outdoors Set pots outdoors 4
when the weather warms. Seedlings will grow
large enough to bloom in three months;
you'll see the results of your hybridizing
effort. Transplant to 6-inch pots or to the
garden and allow plants to continue growing.

cutting flowers

gather ye roses

Part of the joy of growing roses comes when you cut luxurious flowers to extend the pleasure of their presence indoors. Follow a few guidelines to ensure that their beauty and fragrance will last as long as possible.

Cut flowers in early morning or in late afternoon, when they hold the most moisture. Generally, cut long stems if you plan to arrange the roses. Short stems, or no stems, inspire other display methods, such as placing a single stem in a tiny bottle, or floating blooms in an elegant bowl.

Most roses make outstanding cut flowers when they're gathered in the loose bud stage: past tight bud and before their peak of bloom. Tight buds usually don't open after cutting, and fully open blooms don't last. Some rosarians say a rose reaches the ideal stage for cutting when the sepals (the green, leaflike segments that enclose the base of a bud) turn down. When all the sepals have turned down, it's time to cut the flower.

extending the flowers' life

Recut stems indoors (see *bottom* page 73). Before arranging roses, prepare to soak the stems in warm water by removing any leaves and thorns that would be underwater. Extend the life of your cut flowers by adding floral preservative powder (available from florists and crafts stores) to the vase water. Or use a homemade version, combining 1 teaspoon each sugar and bleach with 1 quart of water.

Change the water in the vase every day. Recut stems underwater every two to three days. Keep the arrangement out of direct sun, in a cool location.

roses star

right: **Enjoy the splendor of single rose stems in simple vases. When cutting blooms from first-year roses, it's better to snip short stems.**

pick a stem

left: Be selective when you cut flowers for bouquets. To bolster the strength of a bush and encourage reblooming, cut flower stems for arrangements just above a 5-leaflet leaf. Remove bottom leaves on cut stems before arranging.

fill a basket

left: Gather roses in the morning or in late afternoon. Whisk them indoors and soak the stems in warm water until you're ready to arrange them. Or take a bucket of water to the garden, cut the stems, quickly plunge them into the water, and take them indoors.

always recut

left: Before arranging roses, recut the stems by holding them underwater and cutting off at least 1 to 2 inches. If you don't give the flowers a fresh cut, air bubbles may form in the stems and shorten the life of the blooms.

winter protection

1   **in cold climates** In early fall, stop cutting roses and let plants form hips (seedpods) as they prepare naturally for winter. After the first frost in fall, protect plants from the potential damage caused by freezing and thawing cycles by piling soil over the base of the plant; cover the bud union and up to about 2 feet. Use fresh topsoil or compost, not soil scraped from around the plant.

    Prune overly long canes on bush-type roses to prevent wind damage. Expect a certain amount of winter kill (when canes die as far back as the bud union). Plan to prune off dead canes in early spring.

2   **mulching** After the first hard freeze, pile dry, shredded leaves or bark chips on the mounded soil. In spring, remove the leaves or bark and the pile of soil; spread the leaves and bark around the garden.

3   **extra cold: part one** In areas where winter brings sub-zero temperatures and frigid, drying winds, take extra precautions to help your roses survive. Wrap twine around the canes to hold them erect as you work. Use a garden fork to gently unearth the plant's roots. Dig a trench to one side of the rose large enough to contain the height and width of the plant.

4   **extra cold: part two** Gently tip the plant and lay it in the trench. Cover it with soil. Pile a 2-inch layer of shredded leaves on top of the soil. In early spring, carefully uncover the rose and replant it.

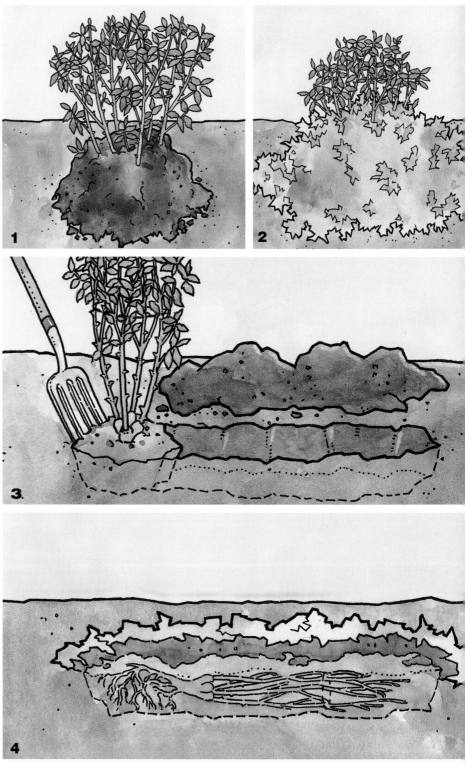

rose cones Roses such as Hybrid Teas need extra protection in cold-winter areas. Purchase a reinforced plastic cylinder or a styrene cone for each plant, if you like. Place the cylinder or cone over the plant and fill it with dry leaves, soil, or bark chips. Remove the protection in early spring.

5

tree rose: part one In mild-winter areas, pile straw around the base of a tree rose (a plant grafted on a tree-length stem). In cold-winter areas, use soil instead of straw. Place a framework of wooden stakes around the tree.

6

tree rose: part two Wrap a generous length of burlap around the stakes to enclose the tree. Secure the fabric using twine or wire. Fill the enclosure with dry leaves or straw. In extremely cold areas, treat tree roses as you would other roses, *opposite*, by burying them in trenches.

7

Overwinter potted tree roses as well as other potted roses by moving them into an unheated garage or to a sheltered place next to the south side of your house. Protect each plant by placing it, pot and all, in a roomy cardboard box and packing the box with shredded newspaper, dry leaves, styrene packing pieces, or peat moss. Surround the box with bales of hay.

Roses in frost-free Zones 9 and 10 seldom need winterizing. Roses in Zone 11 need no protection and do not go dormant; they bloom until you prune them.

bad bugs & good bugs

an ounce of prevention

Healthy roses resist the ravages of insect pests. By focusing on promoting healthy plants, you'll be taking a preventive approach to pests and diseases.

You don't need to arm yourself with an arsenal of toxic products to deal with pests that threaten roses. Instead, use nonchemical troubleshooting methods to prevent and control problems.

Admire your roses up close daily and spot the first signs of pests feeding on stems and buds. Diligently watch for signs of insect invasion, such as discolored or malformed plant parts, holes in leaves, or buds that don't open.

Although it's usually best not to get plants wet, use a hose to blast off some pests, such as aphids, and drown others, such as thrips. A hard spray of water also deters spider mites that live on the undersides of leaves. They're so tiny, you often notice fine webs before you spot the mites. If you must, spray water, insecticidal soap, or other earth-friendly solutions from the top of the rose bush down. Spray the undersides of leaves as well.

aphids

top right: **These voracious pests, usually green, red, or black, blend with buds, stems, and leaves, colonizing before you notice them. Especially fond of tender young shoots and buds, aphids suck plant juices, reducing the plant's vigor. Infested buds usually fail to open. Wash aphids off roses using a spray of water from a hose. For a severe infestation, spray with an insecticidal soap.**

japanese beetles

right: **Adult beetles eat flowers and foliage, deforming and skeletonizing them. To control Japanese beetles, handpick and squish them or knock them into a jar of soapy water. Minimize the population by killing the larval grub form, which lives in lawns. Use a parasitic nematode or milky spore (a bacterium) specific to the grubs.**

thrips

left: These tiny insects spread via the wind and feed mostly on rosebuds. The buds turn brown and do not open, or distorted flowers open with brown edges. Beneficial insects, such as lacewings and damsel bugs, eat thrips. Spray plants using forceful pressure from a hose to drown thrips. Use this method early in the day to allow sun and air to dry plants as quickly as possible.

lady beetles If you encourage their presence, beneficial insects such as lady beetles (otherwise known as ladybugs) work as predators to reduce the population of pests among roses. For the most benefit, scores of beneficial insects must be present, but just a few can make a difference.

Learn to recognize adult and larval forms of beneficial insects, including lady beetles, lacewings, trichogramma wasps, damsel bugs, and others. Attract beneficial insects to your garden by providing nectar-rich plants, such as dill and red clover. Avoid using pesticides, that kill good insects as well as bad ones. Water the garden regularly between rains, and use mulch to keep the soil moist and provide a haven for beneficial microorganisms.

diseases of roses

prevention is key

At some point your roses may become diseased. The most widespread diseases include fiendish-but-not-fatal funguses: black spot, mildew, and rust. Although you cannot completely avoid funguses, good planting and cultural practices help lessen the impact they have in the garden.

Plant roses in sunny locations, where moisture dries quickly from the leaves. Provide good air circulation by spacing plants according to their spread at maturity. Prune Modern roses to an open, vase shape. Crowded canes inhibit adequate air circulation.

Remove unhealthy-looking leaves and buds as soon as you see them. Keep the garden clean. Collect fallen leaves and pruned plant parts from around the base of plants in any season but especially in fall, because most funguses grow, spread, and overwinter in garden debris.

Plant disease-resistant varieties, such as Shrub and Heirloom roses. Few roses boast resistance to black spot, the most prevalent disease of roses. And, remember, resistant does not mean immune.

If, in spite of all your good care, a disease makes a rose look bad by midsummer, prune the plant back by one-half to two-thirds. Pruning forces the shrub to produce new shoots, leaves, and flowers, although this growth won't be as strong as that produced in spring. Wash pruning tools with soap and hot water. Sterilize them with rubbing alcohol to prevent spreading disease.

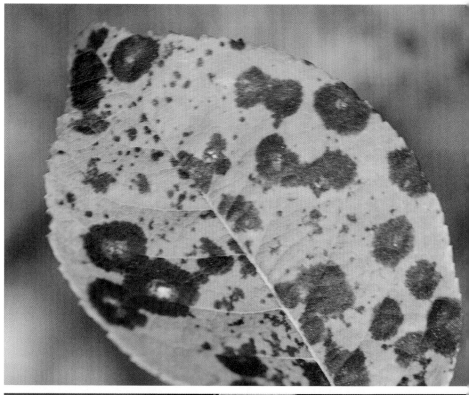

black spot

above right: **Long periods of rainy weather and improper watering promote this fungus. Prevent black spot and rust by spraying plants with a sulfur-based soap solution.**

rust

right: **Cool weather fosters rust. It discolors leaves and defoliates plants. Clean up fallen leaves and spray the plant with fungicidal soap.**

powdery mildew

left: A powdery film appears on leaves affected by this common fungal disease. It strikes roses in most regions during late summer, when humidity and temperatures fluctuate between cool nights and hot days. As a prevention, not a cure, spray roses once a week beginning in midsummer, using a solution of 1 tablespoon of baking powder in 1 gallon of water with a few drops of liquid soap added to help the spray adhere to plant parts. Spray the undersides, as well as the tops of leaves, until thoroughly coated.

other diseases & remedies

disease	symptoms	remedies
botrytis	Gray-brown fuzz on buds. This fungus keeps buds from opening.	Cut and destroy affected parts. Conditions improve in warm, dry weather.
crown gall	Stunted growth and reduced flowering caused by a bacterium. Rough, round growths around roots at or below soil level.	Prune off galls; remove and discard plant in severe cases.
downy mildew	Purplish-red to dark brown spots on leaves; gray fuzz on leaf undersides. This fungus causes defoliation.	Remove and discard affected leaves. Use baking soda spray as for powdery mildew.
mosaic	Viruses displayed in discolored patterns on leaves.	Symptoms usually disappear on their own. If not, remove and destroy plant.

tools

well-stocked shed

Tools for tending roses last for years if you clean them after each use and sharpen them regularly. A dull tool not only makes your work more difficult and time-consuming, it also hurts the plants.

Invest in premium, well-made tools and save yourself the aggravation of perpetually replacing inexpensive ones.

For pruning bushes and cutting blooms, hand pruners, loppers, pruning saws, and shears–or flower snips–occupy first place in a rosarian's toolshed.

tooling up

right: In addition to hand tools, stock your garden shed with a long-handled spade, a garden fork, and a cultivator. Keep plant markers, a dethorner, and a sprayer handy, too. Have buckets for carrying fertilizer as well as cut flowers. Wear boots, gloves, and a hat to protect yourself as you work in the garden.

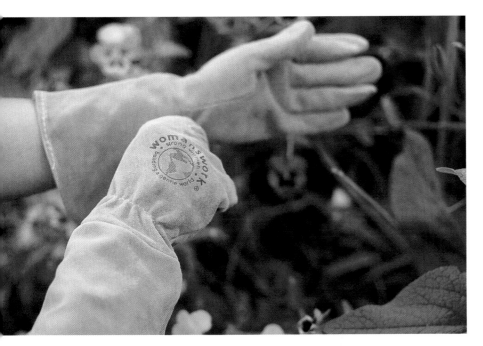

gauntlet time

left: When you work around roses, with their thorns and prickles, protect your skin by wearing a pair of heavy-duty gloves. Gauntlet-style gloves extend past the wrist and cover part of your arm. Those made from leather or another impenetrable material allow you to dethorn the roses you cut for arrangements by sliding your gloved fingers down the stems.

versatile twine

Left below: Use twine to tie rose canes as you train them to grow on fences, arbors, and obelisks. In late fall, wrap twine around long canes to keep them from blowing and breaking in winter winds. Also use it to secure burlap wraps on tree roses. Twine deteriorates eventually and needs to be replaced.

pruning device

Below: Choose bypass pruners that cut like scissors and slice easily through less bulky rose canes. Avoid anvil-type pruners, the blades which meet when they close; they could crush canes. Use a pruning saw to cut canes that are thicker than your little finger. Keep a sharpening tool on hand to hone cutting blades after each use.

in the garden

in the
garden

Roses make outstanding plants for any landscape, whether large or small. Tougher than they appear, roses are as dependable as they are versatile, wherever you live and whatever the style of your home and garden. When you choose roses for your landscape, you'll find ones to fulfill many purposes, both functional and aesthetic. They'll even help you resolve the challenges of your yard.

style considerations Roses are associated with times past, but they look as much at home in a contemporary or urban setting as in a cottage or country landscape. To select a rose to fit the style of your home and garden, consider its growth habit and potential size as well as its bloom color, bloom time, and hardiness.

Standards, or tree forms, and pillar roses harmonize well with contemporary designs, as do some of the once-blooming Heirloom roses. After flowering, they blend with the garden and other shrubs. Arbors dripping with lush blooms, such as the entry bedecked with 'Cécile Brünner' *opposite*, recall Victorian designs of a century ago but create a timeless impact. Whether planted in mixed borders or in beds of their own, roses harmonize with any garden style.

landscaping goals Roses climb, sprawl, and ramble. They grow tall and upright or small and compact. The kinds of roses you choose depend in large part on which area of the landscape you want to decorate or ameliorate. Rambling or quickly spreading roses, for example, become gorgeous groundcovers that help you cope with a steep slope.

Large roses, such as Albas, Grandifloras, and Rugosas, work in small as well as large spaces. They make impressive specimens whether you plant them in a shrub border or set them apart in a bed of their own. Rugosas form prickly, impenetrable hedges that shield the yard from the street, providing privacy and security.

Smaller yards call for appropriately sized plants. This is where Miniatures and Floribundas as well as many Polyanthas and Shrub roses strut their stuff. These compact growers work to accent rather than overwhelm an area, wheether you plant them along a walk or in a pot.

Get to know many types of roses, and then match their personalities and attributes to a task. You'll soon discover the best roses for your yard.

roses with perennials

designing beds and borders

Roses form the heart of harmonious compositions in a garden. Low-growing or climbing, stately or sprawling, use roses to provide eye-catching focal points or restrained accents for surrounding perennials, depending on their growth habits.

Edge a bed or border with petite roses, such as Miniatures, Polyanthas, and Flower Carpet varieties. Combine tall roses, which often lose their lower leaves by midsummer, with low-growing, bushy perennials. Or use tall, sturdy roses as supports for vining plants. Vine partners, such as clematis or wisteria, extend the flowering season through the summer. This is important if you plant Heirloom roses that bloom once early in the growing season. Group roses and perennials in duos or trios that bloom at the same time for spectacular results.

sunny combination

above right: **English roses form a backdrop for a sunny border of lady's mantle, silvery lamb's-ears, cranesbill, and bellflower. Contrasting flower colors and foliage shapes contribute to long-season interest.**

three-part harmony

right: **Clematis wends its way through a border planting of bellflower and a fragrant 'Graham Thomas' (English) rose. The muted colors make a natural combination. Group trios of compatible plants throughout the garden for pleasing results.**

When planting roses, leave room on all sides so they can reach full size without crowding. This also permits air circulation between plants, which helps prevent disease. When designing plantings, picture a rose at its mature size and plan accordingly. Determine the height and spread of any rose before you buy it.

Plant perennials of staggered heights in formal borders or paired in informal groupings; create a tiered effect with shorter plants in front of taller ones. Roses mix as well with foliage plants as they do with bloomers. Combine them with a variety of textural perennials, ornamental grasses, and shrubs.

cottage garden

left: **Vibrant shades of blue and pink perennials, including foxglove, delphinium, poppy, and bellflower, create an English country garden look that complements the rose clambering up and over the arbor.**

rose companions

Whether married happily or just friends, the best plant pairs complement each other. Combined with other plants, roses make ideal partners that add height, fragrance, and sometimes season-long bloom. Consider these characteristics, as well as roses' overall shape and foliage color, when pairing them with other plants (including other roses). For example, reddish barberry, silvery artemisia, and chartreuse coleus cohabitate strikingly with rose foliage, which varies from green to gray to burgundy. Textured lamb's-ears, dwarf evergreens, and lady's mantle make rich combinations as well.

Harmonize bloom colors in similar or complementary hues, or set up striking contrasts between opposites. A multitude of plants get along famously with roses, whether they bloom together, or bloom at different times, or don't bloom at all. Choose your favorite annuals and perennials–as well as herbs, vegetables, and shrubs–for rose companions based on their ability to enhance rather than compete.

pest deterrents

Alliums, including garlic, onions, chives, and ornamental varieties deter aphids and other pests when you plant them around roses. Plant allium

places please
above right: **Low-growing, large-leaf bergenias stand out against a backdrop of roses and add to the overall layered look of roses and perennials.**

pretty pest prevention
right: **Allium multibulbosum and 'Penelope' (Hybrid Musk) cozy up to each other. Alliums, including garlic and chives, make especially good companions for roses because they provide a natural defense against aphids.**

bulbs in fall and enjoy their blossoms the following spring or summer.

Many plants that attract beneficial insects to the garden look good with roses, too. Queen Anne's lace, dill, candytuft, parsley, and fennel, among others, serve as magnets to good bugs that feast on pests.

subtle contrast
above left: Cranesbill *(Geranium pratense)* and 'Mrs. Robb's' euphorbia contrast beautifully with the blooms of 'New Dawn' (Climber). Most successful plant partners share the same cultural needs, such as sun, moisture, and soil fertility.

pinks on parade
left: Bicolored pinks *(Dianthus)* and delicate thyme bloom in perfect harmony at the foot of 'Earth Song' (Grandiflora). Herbs and roses make happy companions, with their contrasting textures and irresistible fragrances.

great rose companions

artemisia	hollyhock
aster	iris
coreopsis	lavender
delphinium	lemon balm
foxglove	sage
garden phlox	shasta daisy
geranium (perennial and annual)	strawberry
	sweet alyssum

roses with roses

all of a kind

Once you start growing roses, the next thing you know, you're collecting them. Although planting an entire garden with one type of rose issues an invitation to pests and diseases, setting a group of various roses in a bed of their own increases their chances for thriving. When you combine roses, maximize their strengths by congregating varieties. Try amassing groundcover roses. Plant potentially head-high Shrub roses to form a hedge or screen.

Be creative in putting together a collection. Select roses that were introduced in the same years as your family members' birthdays, for instance. Collect white-flowering roses with different characteristics: red stamens, yellow stamens, single petals, double petals, and so on.

Combine roses according to their size and bloom time. Place large, once-blooming Heirloom roses at the back of a bed, where their dark foliage and dense growth take over when flowering stops. They provide a green backdrop for smaller, everblooming roses. Set Miniatures at the front edge of the bed to complete the tiered effect.

dress up a site

above right: **Build raised beds for your rose collection if the soil drains poorly. Make the garden more attractive by edging it with large stones native to your area.**

dazzling placement

right: **A display garden at Heirloom Roses in St. Paul, Oregon, presents glorious plants along with garden design ideas. Adapt these ideas to your garden by planting Climbers and Ramblers on tuteurs—as shown here with white 'Venusta Pendula,' red 'Altissimo,' and pink 'Newport Fairy.' Copy the idea of nestling a weathered bench into shrubby 'Général Jacqueminot' (Hybrid Perpetual).**

wondrous heights

left: Stunning scents and colors greet anyone passing through this gate as 'Cécile Brünner' (Polyantha) and 'Zéphirine Drouhin' (Bourbon) climb over the garden wall. 'Frau Dagmar Hartopp' a compact Rugosa, presents its single, fragrant flowers in a waist-high display that brightens with rose hips in autumn. Combining roses of varying types and heights creates a complete effect: overhead, nose high, and at your fingertips.

roses as edgings

front and center

Trim, compact roses fit in along the edges of beds and borders, lending a neat finishing touch there. Miniature roses are the obvious choice for edging a border, sidewalk, or garden path. They offer reliable, steadfast color from early summer to fall.

Polyanthas and some of the smaller Landscape roses, such as Flower Carpet and Meidiland varieties, represent other compact edging possibilities that provide dense clusters of blooms almost continuously. Trim the plants regularly to keep them from wandering into pathways and snagging the ankles of passersby.

compact color
right: **'The Fairy' (Polyantha) edges a perennial bed with its soft pink blooms and blends marvelously with sage, lamb's-ears, and catmint.**

edge your beds

left: Roses cascade over the stacked stone edge of a garden path. Combined with low-growing evergreens and deciduous shrubs, they form a colorful, low-maintenance garden with year-round interest. Landscape roses make the perfect choices for this large garden, where they have plenty of room to spread.

low-down beauty

left: A classic mixed border displays the many faces of roses. They edge the bed as fittingly as they fill in between the perennials, and make a strong backdrop, too. Bordering a fence, a wall, or an invisible property line, the graduated sizes create a sense of seclusion.

roses as hedges

boundary beauties

Plant a row of roses to fulfill a variety of landscaping functions: mark the perimeter of your property, surround a garden area, create a microclimate for tender plants, provide a sense of seclusion around a patio or deck, or serve as an impenetrable deterrent to unwanted visitors. You get that, plus a fragrant, living fence too. Choose tall, wickedly thorny roses, such as Rugosas, when planting to create a security hedge.

Stagger planting holes to create a fuller, less-contrived look and, at the same time, allow room for air to circulate among the roses. Space quick growers, such as Rugosas and Shrubs, 3 to 4 feet apart; plant Floribundas and other upright roses about 2 feet apart. When outlining a garden or a part of the yard, such as a curbside or walkway, place roses in single file. Select roses that reach the same height.

mix it up

above: Heirloom roses, including the deep pink 'Archiduc Joseph' (Tea) and creamy pink 'Felicia' (Hybrid Musk), combine well with evergreen shrubs, such as the pittosporum in this hedge.

awesome aroma

right: 'Celsiana' (Damask), with its intensely fragrant flowers, forms a 5-foot-tall, broadly spreading canopy that creates privacy in a corner of the garden.

lazy lushness

left: A sturdy picket fence gives 'New Dawn' (Climber) all the support it needs to spread into a gorgeous hedge. Ramblers, such as 'American Pillar' and 'Albéric Barbier,' also drape a fence elegantly. Install vinyl fencing and save yourself from regular painting chores.

down in front

below: Amass a broad lineup of just about any compact and bushy rose variety that reaches 3 to 4 feet tall to make a handsome hedge that's tidy enough for a front yard. Select from a number of rose classes, including Shrub, Landscape, Floribunda, or Grandiflora. Mix roses with similar-size shrubs that bear various foliage colors for a tapestry effect.

roses with fences

classic combo

Roses and fences go together like peaches and cream. Fences provide a perfect place to train climbing and rambling roses. But they also offer enough support for any other rose with long canes. Let roses grow over and through fence slats for an informal look. Train and trim them for a more formal design.

Plant roses along a fence either to accent the design of the structure (assuming it's attractive) or to camouflage it. Hide a chain-link fence by tying canes loosely to the wires; guide the canes in a fan shape until they reach the top of the fence. If you plant at each fence post, guide canes to the left and right of the post somewhat horizontally. Combining roses with vines, grasses, perennials, or evergreen shrubs are other good ways to hide a fence.

before roses
above: **This charming picket fence garden realizes its full potential when the roses clamber over the rebar arches above it, as shown** *opposite top.*

rustic rails
right: **Perennials and roses spill over both sides of a split-rail fence, enhancing its simple design.**

after roses

left: 'Constance Spry,' the first of the David Austin English roses, graces the rebar arches and makes a magnificent scallop above the fence line. The design provides privacy for the yard beyond, but it also frames a window to the street from the other side of the fence. The fence posts make sturdy supports for upright roses such as the large yellow bloomer.

dual magnetism

left: Train a rose on a framed section of lattice fence to separate one part of a garden from another or to provide privacy next to a deck or patio. Once-flowering 'Alchymist' (Shrub) possesses great vigor, growing 6 to 8 feet tall. To extend the flower show, combine it with a repeat bloomers such as 'Galway Bay' (Floribunda).

climbing on supports

wall hangings

Take your roses and your garden to greater heights. Give Climbers, Ramblers, and other roses more than 4 feet tall the support they need to reach their potential by training them to a structure, such as an arbor, pergola, or trellis.

Structures add handsome and long-lasting architectural elements to the landscape. When embellished with roses, they become magnificent focal points. Train roses up a wall, along a roof, or into a tree. Guide them over entries, porches, and windows. Use the versatile nature of roses to soften hard angles and to hide eyesores, such as a dilapidated building or a compost pile.

cover up

right: **'American Pillar' (Rambler) scales a house with the assistance of trellis-work attached to the walls and roof.**

heavy-duty needs

above left: 'Dr. W. Van Fleet' (Rambler) needs a sturdy support, such as the corner of a house. A delicate trellis wouldn't hold up under its mature weight. This plant is guided by wires achored near the base of the plant and attached to the soffit with eye screws.

modular means

above right: Artful trellises, such as this modular set, compose a pleasing view on a once-uninteresting blank wall. One rose plant (in training) climbs the supports without hiding them.

extra warmth

left: Fragrant, once-blooming 'May Queen' (Rambler) tolerates cold but benefits from the shelter and warmth provided by a stone wall.

arbors

Use a graceful arbor to frame a view or create an impressive entry for a garden or walkway. Add a gate for a sense of privacy as well as anticipation. Extend the old-fashioned design that many arbors bring to a yard by joining a fence to it. Place an arbor with a seat at the end of a path or in the garden as a destination.

Depending on its design and material, an arbor lends contemporary or traditional style to a garden. Materials range from wood (redwood, cedar, or twig) and vinyl to plastic-coated steel, cast iron, and other metals.

Climbing roses usually begin to take off by their third year. Training them requires patience to bend the canes and gently guide them to fit a structure. Depending on the rose, it will smother an arbor within a few more years.

extended bloom

above: **Combine fragrant roses that bloom only once a year with a fall-blooming vine such as an autumn-blooming clematis to extend the season of color and scent in a garden.**

queen of climbers

right: **Few Climbers rival 'New Dawn' for the lush blooms that cover the plant in late spring and appear sporadically into fall. A fast grower, it envelops an arbor. Plant one slow-growing Climber on each side of an arbor.**

patriotic appeal

left: 'America' (Climber) greets visitors with its bodacious blooms and spicy clove fragrance as it blankets a sturdy but romantic-looking arbor. Paired with a gated fence, the structure makes an impressive entryway. This large (more than 5-foot-wide) arbor provides enough space to frame a sidewalk and allow two to walk side by side. Use a 3- to 4-foot-wide arbor for secondary paths and garden entrances.

climbing on supports

pergolas & pillars

Other types of supports, such as pergolas, pillars, and trellises, give you more ways to twist and coax roses into picturesque displays. Pergolas suit rampant vines; you need to anchor the posts securely in the ground by burying them 18 to 24 inches deep in cement. Pergolas look equally impressive abutting a house wall, shading a garden walk, or framing an outdoor dining area.

Look for other imaginative ways to train your roses: on a pillar or a post, an old clothesline or ladder, an iron railing, or a rattan headboard.

rambunctious roses

right: Fast-growing Ramblers clamber on a sturdy fence, while 'Albéric Barbier,' also a Rambler, grows up and over an umbrella form that gives it sturdy support. Fashion a similar support by attaching a large bicycle wheel to the top of a post.

raising canes

left: Rough wood pergolas add rustic charm and dappled shade to a garden walk. 'Fun Jwan Lo' (Shrub) could be planted at the posts and intertwined with wisteria for a more everblooming effect. Loosely tether roses to their support, using strips of old nylon stocking or plastic; avoid using wire, which could damage the plants.

upright roses

left: Roses that reach 4 to 6 feet tall, such as this 'John Cabot' (Shrub), need support. This heavy-duty pillar works well for upright roses. Choose a structure that suits your garden's style, from wood obelisks or bamboo tripods to wire tutuers or steel stakes.

roses | **103**

a fan-shape trellis

you will need

³⁄₄×1¹⁄₂ in. lath:
six 84 in. long
two 96 in. long
one 12 in. long
one 16 in. long

4×4×84-in. posts

³⁄₄×1¹⁄₂×16 in.
³⁄₄×1¹⁄₂×25 in.

³⁄₄×3¹⁄₂×12 in.
³⁄₄×3¹⁄₂×32 in.

³⁄₄×7¹⁄₄×25 in.

³⁄₄×10×24 in.

³⁄₄×³⁄₄×27 in.

³⁄₈×³⁄₄×³⁄₄ in.

1¹⁄₄-in. deck screws

2-in. deck screws

drill

screwdriver

skillsaw

plant support

Build a classic-shape trellis of long-lasting cedar to highlight a spectacular rose. A series of trellises could form a backdrop for a garden, separate one area of a garden from another, or create privacy as well as attractive supports for plants. The trellis shown stands one foot away from the fence to allow air circulation around the plants. The trellises are held upright by 4×4 supports.

Cut all the pieces before assembling any of them. Build the trellis on a flat, level surface. If you plan to build a series of trellises, keep in mind that you don't need end posts for each one. Two trellises placed side by side, for example, would require three–rather than four–posts. Using 4×4s as posts, set two trellises at right angles to make a handsome corner and frame an area. Finish the structures using exterior paint or stain.

happy pair

right: **Clematis montana rubens and roses, such as bright red 'Dortmund' and white 'Alba,' go together well with the trellises. Paired with the fence, they serve as a beautiful backdrop for a perennial garden.**

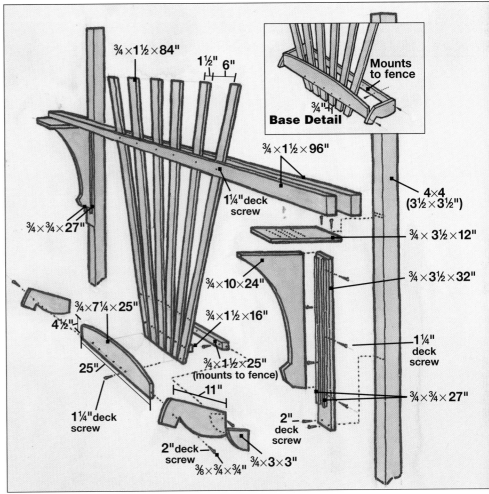

¾×1½×84"

1½" 6"

Mounts to fence

¾"

Base Detail

¾×1½×96"

4×4 (3½×3½")

1¼" deck screw

¾×¾×27"

¾×3½×12"

¾×10×24"

¾×3½×32"

¾×7¼×25"

4½"

¾×1½×16"

1¼" deck screw

25"

¾×1½×25" (mounts to fence)

¾×¾×27"

1¼" deck screw

11"

2" deck screw

2" deck screw

⅜×¾×¾"

¾×3×3"

pretty support

left: A fan-shape trellis provides decorative support for a climbing rose. Because the structure's design is an important part of the overall look, use roses that grow slowly, not rampantly, so they don't cover the trellis completely.

roses on slopes

floriferous groundcovers

Broad stretches of land, steep banks, and sloping terrain present landscaping challenges. Transform these common problems into assets, using roses to blanket the land with their beauty and grip the soil with their roots, thereby helping control erosion. Deal with steep slopes by planting roses in terraced beds.

Use Climbers (both standard and Miniature varieties), Floribundas, and Landscape roses, such as Meidiland and Flower Carpet, in mass plantings as groundcovers. Landscape and Shrub roses, especially, represent tough, disease-resistant, and easy-care plants. To keep Climbers growing close to the ground, peg their canes down at intervals.

Even though roses are deciduous (dropping most of their leaves in late fall), they retain a winter presence and add an acrobatic aesthetic to the landscape with their tangled, sometimes twiggy, growth.

mini mass

above right: The small-flowered climbing Miniature 'Nozomi' trails over rocky ground and forms an attractive groundcover where little else grows.

streams of roses

right: Pergolas festooned with climbers, including 'Madame Ernest Calvat' and 'Zépherine Drouhin,' join masses of Floribundas in stone-edged beds to turn an ordinary hillside into a resplendent scene.

weed prevention

above: The red-flowered 'Max Graf,' a hybrid Rugosa, makes a low-growing landscape shrub. Its long canes and prolific, rich green leaves make it a good candidate for use as a groundcover on a sunny bank or hillside. The thick growth helps to shade out weeds in summer. The canes root where they touch soil, so the rose spreads naturally.

rosy stairs

left: What was once a treacherous, difficult-to-manage slope has been transformed into a lovely outdoor room. Roses bedeck the steps up the hill to a pergola-topped terrace. The bloomers also surround the pergola and have begun to climb it.

roses as standards

unusual trees

Whether you call it a standard, a tree rose, or a patio rose, the treelike rose form makes an impressive show. Use standards to flank an entry to the house or a garden, display one as a specimen, or plant them in containers and enjoy their versatile portability.

Miniature standards grow on a trunk stock between 18 and 20 inches tall. Regular standards grow on stock up to 36 inches tall. Because the bud union, or graft, is at the top of the long trunk (not buried in the ground), the plants need extra protection over winter in Zones 6 and colder.

Prune standards the way you do bush roses. Cut off diseased or dead canes. Remove any suckers that grow on the rootstock and the trunk stock, close to their base. Trim the top periodically to keep it rounded.

standard fare

above: One of the advantages of growing standards is that they typically display their flowers head high, allowing room for perennials and annuals clamber at their feet.

tiny trees

right: Any Miniature rose, from 'Black Jade' and 'Cupcake' to 'Minnie Pearl' or 'Starina,' works well as a potted standard.

point of entry

above: In containers or in the ground, Floribundas, such as 'Showbiz,' make outstanding sentinels at an entry to the garden. As an alternative form, weeping standards feature roses with lax canes, such as 'Sea Foam' (Shrub) and 'Nozomi' (a miniature Climber). In cold climates, tree-form roses must be protected with insulated wraps or by moving them to a sheltered location.

roses for small places

petite delights

Even in the smallest gardens, it's possible to grow healthy, beautiful roses. Success depends on the type of rose you choose and how you use it. Countless roses from a variety of classes, including Miniatures, Polyanthas, and Floribundas, suit small spaces. An ever-growing array of Landscape roses also presents gorgeous options for limited spaces.

As long as there's room for their roots to grow, roses conform well to tight spots, whether edging a sidewalk or driveway, filling a pocket in a foundation planting or a corner, gracing a container, or climbing a wall. Use the vertical space in small areas by putting a Climber to work there.

above standard

right: Trimmed into a neat standard, a young 'Gertrude Jekyll' (English) takes to life in a pot. It offers a portable spot of color and cheer for a deck, balcony, or patio.

grow up

left: 'Hi Ho,' a climbing Miniature, grows happily on a support in a wood planter. Use walls or an arbor to train climbers efficiently in a small space. Choose from an always-expanding retinue of Miniatures in climbing form, such as 'Climbing Rainbow's End,' 'Red Cascade,' and 'Snowfall.'

hang it

below left: Put a few touches of color anywhere—on the house or garage wall, or on a deck or wood fence—by hanging pots or wire baskets filled with Miniature roses. Mix colors or use just one color per pot. Remember that overhanging eaves may prevent containers from receiving the sun and rain they need, so put them on the sunniest side of the house and be prepared to water even when it rains. Both climbing and bushy Miniatures make good candidates for baskets.

on edge

below right: Edge small gardens with the most diminutive Miniatures, such as 'Tom Thumb.' Their dainty appearance belies their hardiness, especially because most grow on their own roots. When planted along a walkway, they even stand up to the weight of shoveled snow piled on them.

container growing

Just as you need to dig the proper size hole for a rose you plant in the ground, so you need to select the right-size container for a rose you grow in a pot. Miniatures fit in small (1- to 5-gallon) pots but full-size bushes, such as Floribundas and Shrub roses, require larger tubs–up to 18 inches across and 24 inches deep. Half-barrels and other wood or composition tubs make excellent planters.

Any rose adapts to container planting as long as there's plenty of room for root growth. Using a lightweight potting mix makes your portable pots easier to move around. Enrich the soil with compost and peat moss; sprinkle in water-retentive crystals. Feed plants weekly throughout the growing season. Water when the soil feels dry (daily during hot, dry weather).

In cold climates, move pots to an unheated garage or basement over winter.

great roses for containers

'China Doll'	**Miniatures:**
'Duchess of Portland'	'Black Jade'
'Flower Carpet'	'Child's Play'
'Hermosa'	'Dresden Doll'
'Jean Mermet'	'Jean Kenneally'
'Margo Koster'	'Minnie Pearl'
'Petite de Hollande'	'Starina'
'Rose de Meaux'	'Sunblaze'
'Rose de Rescht'	'Teddy Bear'

little ones indoors

above: Use potted roses, such as 'Small Miracle,' temporarily indoors to decorate for a special occasion. Keep them in a sunny window until moving them to the garden.

flowers anywhere

right: Petite roses make pretty accents when decorating outdoor living areas.

extra care

left: Young roses benefit from the extra care they receive when potted for their first season in your garden. Disguised by sturdy baskets, pots of 'The Fairy' (Polyantha) thrive and bloom through the summer in a plant stand. Transplanted to the garden at the end of summer, the roses have time to develop new roots before winter.

from the garden

from the
garden

conjure up memories of your garden year-round. Enjoy transforming the blooms from your roses into other lasting treasures, such as rose beads, by trying your hand at an old-fashioned floral craft.

capture the essence As a symbol of love and beauty, the rose and its beguiling fragrance has aroused passions since the days of Cleopatra and Mark Antony. You, too, can languish in a hot bath redolent of roses, letting their delicate perfume envelop you, as did the ancient Egyptians. Concoct your own beauty treatments and slather roses on your skin in the form of a cooling splash or a soothing facial.

In between the times of the ancient Romans and Queen Victoria, roses were prized as much for their sweet flavor and medicinal value as for their beauty and fragrance. Just as fragrant rose petals were picked and pummeled into tasty syrups and candies, jellies and beverages then, you can put them to use in the kitchen today.

Our love affair with roses continues as it has throughout history, and it's no wonder. The most venerated of flowers offers infinite uses as well as pleasures beyond the garden. The more roses you grow, the more ways you'll find to use them in a variety of ways: decorative, fragrant, cosmetic, and culinary.

gather the beauty Fresh-picked roses make splendid bouquets, wreaths, and other decorations with their enchanting scent and beauty. Even when dried, the petals offer subtle scents, especially if they're combined with spices in aromatic sachets. These sweet-scented bundles, laid among linens or clothing,

Discover the astonishing flavors and varied uses of rose petals and hips (the fruity and nutritious seedpods) in culinary delicacies. Turn fresh petals into sparkling, sugar-dusted garnishes for desserts or tea sandwiches. Or capture the ethereal essence of roses in a cool drink that's the perfect refreshment after working in the garden.

Use only roses that have not been treated with toxic chemicals; and do not use florist roses in cooking. Otherwise, be imaginative and see how many different ways you can find to savor the beauty and fragrance of roses.

decorating with roses

rose bouquets

A beautiful array of dizzyingly fragrant roses never fails to please, whether you gather a handful or an armload. A classic bouquet combines colors, shapes, and forms in a rich tapestry of blooms. Experiment with your choice of container, but keep it simple so it won't overpower the flowers.

Couple roses with other flowers, such as columbine, iris, salvia, and lilies, for different looks. To round out a pretty mixed bouquet, add greenery, including leaves of lady's mantle, hosta, lemon balm, and fern. Tuck in fillers, such as sprigs of artemisia or eucalyptus, for a finishing touch.

inviting scene
right: **A cut glass vase holds peppermint-striped 'Variegata di Bologna' (Bourbon) and rich pink 'Madame Berkeley' (Tea).**

autumn combo

left: As summer turns to fall, enjoy a final bouquet, such as sunny 'Graham Thomas' blooms combined with fat hips of 'Eglantine' in a porcelain pitcher.

the nose knows

below left: Old roses balance their limited array of colors with an astonishing variety of perfumes, from musk and citrus to spice and a pure rose essence. Bouquets such as this capture an extraordinary perfume in a vase.

roses on stage

below right: Go for the surprise element. Who would think that a moss-lined wire urn could hold a big bouquet of roses? You would, if you were to tuck an ordinary jar full of water inside the urn. The moss hides the jar, and the arrangement looks good in any setting.

decorating with roses

wreaths and more

Hang a wreath of fresh roses on a wall or use it as a tabletop centerpiece. Make a beautiful ring of fresh or dried roses in one or two contrasting colors. If you like, tuck in other blooms (fresh or dried), such as hydrangea or allium.

Hang your rose wreath away from light and heat to preserve its beauty. Avoid hanging such a delicate creation on a door, where it could be damaged.

For a special occasion, fashion dainty wreaths into napkin rings or circlets to be slipped around the base of pillar candles for table decorations. Twist wire around the stems of Miniature roses and bend the wired stems.

delicate delight

right: **This wreath of 'Cameo' (Polyantha) roses will look stunningly fresh for up to a week. It will dry gradually and continue to look pretty for months.**

1 preparation Use a 12-inch-diameter floral foam ring as a wreath base. You'll need five to six dozen partially open, fresh or dried roses (about 1½ inches wide), 19-gauge florist's wire, floral tape, and twenty ¾-inch prewired silver baubles. If you use fresh flowers, soak the floral foam ring in water and place it on a flat, waterproof work surface. For dried roses, omit the soaking.

2 design Trim rose stems to 1 inch and push them into the wreath base. Completely cover the ring with flowers. If necessary, strengthen rose stems by twisting 3-inch-long pieces of 19-gauge wire around them, forming a wire stem. Wrap the stem with floral tape to cover the wire. Insert the wire stems of silver baubles here and there around the ring. Keep the base of a fresh-rose wreath moist by soaking it every few days in a sink full of warm water for five minutes.

drying flowers

Pick partially open blooms; cut stems to 1 inch. Pour a 1-inch layer of a drying agent, such as silica gel (a crystalline dessicant), in an airtight container with a lid. Stand each rose in the silica gel. Cover the roses with silica gel by pouring it gently over each bloom, sifting it in between the petals with your fingers. Cover the container. Carefully uncover the roses when dry (within a week for most blooms; four days for Miniatures).

the scent of roses

reason for roses

The fragrance of roses is equally compelling whether you sit outdoors under a bower of flowers and bask in their perfume or gather petals and bring them indoors to make a spicy sachet for dresser drawers.

As you stroll among the aromatic blooms in the garden and snip them for bouquets, bury your face among the petals, breathe deeply, and enjoy the soothing effect.

The scent of roses is determined by their genes and varies from faint and elusive to heady and intoxicating. As complex as any perfume, rose fragrance echoes apple, citrus, honey, myrrh, musk, and raspberry, evoking descriptions of sweet, spicy, and fruity.

number one scent

right: Some gardeners regard 'Madame Isaac Pereire' (Bourbon) as the most fragrant rose of all. It retains its color and scent when dried for potpourri and sachets.

rose sachets

This rosy blend combines the subtle perfume of dried rose petals with aromatic spices and essential oils (available at craft or herb stores). Place sachets in closets and drawers to impart their scent among sheets, towels, and clothing. When making sachets, begin with exquisitely fragrant roses, such as 'Blanc Double de Coubert,' 'Double Delight,' 'Fragrant Cloud,' 'Madame Alfred Carriére,' and 'Sombreuil.'

   large glass or ceramic bowl
 8 cups dried rose petals
 1 ounce ground cinnamon
 1 ounce ground mace
 ½ ounce ground cloves
 12 tonka beans (powdered in a coffee grinder or
   spice mill)
   essential oils of rose and musk
   1-gallon wide mouth glass jar
   fabric
   ribbon

In a large glass or ceramic bowl, combine the rose petals, spices, and tonka beans. Add 20 drops each of the rose and musk essential oils. Stir well. Place the mix in a 1-gallon wide-mouth glass jar. Store the jar in a dark place for three weeks to allow the sachet mix to age. Shake the jar daily to blend the contents.

   Make sachets by placing ¼ cup of the mix in the center of a 6-inch square of fabric. (Use scraps of cotton, linen, or other breathable cloth. Cut the fabric with pinking shears, for a decorative edge.) Draw up the corners of the fabric to form a pouch. Tie a 12-inch length of ribbon around the gathered neck of the pouch. Repeat for each square. This recipe makes a dozen sachets.

sachet candidates

top: **To dry roses for crafting, harvest flowers early in the day, after the dew has evaporated. Lay them on a screen or a rack in a warm, dark, airy place until crisp.**

rosy posterity

above: **Sachets preserve roses' tantalizing scents and diffuse them among stored clothes or linens.**

roses for beauty

mixed blessings

Over the centuries, people have transformed roses into concoctions for bath and beauty regimens as well as medicines. Cleopatra and the ancient Romans scattered rose petals in their famous baths, believing in their power to preserve youth and beauty. According to old herbals, roses were widely grown and gathered in Medieval and Renaissance times to treat a range of maladies, from headaches to "a loose belly and the spitting of blood." Although you may not take an infusion of roses for nervousness today, you might enjoy the soothing qualities that fragrant petals impart to a bath or their astringent properties in a facial. Roses remain valued components for popular cosmetics as well as homemade beauty and bath products.

Rosewater, first made in the 10th century to cure the spitting of blood, remains an important ingredient in fine soaps and perfumes. It's one of the easiest ways to capture the essence of roses from your garden. Soak a cloth in chilled rosewater, and place it on your forehead for a while to relieve a headache caused by being out in the sun too long.

homemade rosewater

right: Place 1½ cups bottled spring water, 2 tablespoons vodka, and 1½ cups fresh fragrant rose petals in a clean 1-quart glass jar. Store the jar in the refrigerator for 1 week; shake it daily. Strain out the rose petals and pour the rosewater into a bottle or atomizer. Spritz or splash it on your skin. Rosewater keeps 2 weeks in the refrigerator.

spa-quality facial

left: Make a delightful mud mask that both cleanses and soothes your face. Mix equal parts powdered cosmetic clay (green, red, or white) and either rosewater or distilled water until a smooth paste forms. If the paste is too thin, add a bit of powdered clay; if it's too thick, add sprinkles of water. Stir in a handful of minced rose petals (just-picked and sweet-scented). Mix well. Apply the mask to your face, avoiding the delicate skin around your eyes. Relax and allow the mask to dry (15 to 20 minutes). Rinse it off by splashing your face with warm water, then cool.

romantic bath

left: Make your own aromatherapy bath by scattering rose petals and other botanicals, such as lemon balm and scented-geranium leaves, in the bathwater. Add fern fronds and hydrangea blossoms for a romantic touch.

rose beads

time	skill
10 days	easy

you will need

- 4 cups dried rose petals
- coffee or spice mill
- cast–iron pot
- bottled rosewater
- 2–quart glass or porcelain bowl
- ¼ cup flour
- essential oil of rose
- large plate or tray
- carpet thread
- darning needle
- coat hanger
- beading thread

special charm

Enjoy this craft of years gone by, using roses from a special occasion, such as a wedding or a birthday. Alternate the earthy, handmade rose beads with other pretty beads, if you like. When not in use, store the beads in a drawer as a delicate sachet.

rosy beads

right: **When you wear rose beads against your skin, your body warmth releases their light, sweet scent.**

1 **make mash** Dry the rose petals in a warm, dark, airy place until they are brittle. Pulverize the petals in a coffee or spice mill until they're finely powdered.

In a cast-iron pot, blend the rose petal powder with enough rosewater to make a mash. Simmer on the stove for 30 minutes, stirring often. Add rosewater as needed to prevent scorching. Repeat the simmering process three days in a row, leaving the mash in the pot from day to day. The mash will gradually react with the iron and turn black.

Place the mash in a glass or porcelain bowl. Blend in the flour to form a dough. If you don't shape the beads right away, cover the dough and store it in the refrigerator for up to three days.

2 **form beads** To shape beads, pinch off bits of dough; roll them between your thumb and forefinger into smooth, pea-size spheres. Dab your fingertips with rose essential oil to intensify the beads' fragrance as you shape them. Set the finished beads on a large plate.

String the beads onto 15-inch lengths of carpet thread, knotted at one end, using a darning needle. Push the needle through the center of each bead; slide the bead onto the thread. Tie strands of beads to the bottom of a hanger; knot each strand to secure it. Hang the beads to dry in a warm, dark place. Each day, gently slide the beads up and down each thread to prevent them from sticking to it. Beads dry completely in a week to 10 days. Restring on beading thread in desired length. Attach a clasp or tie the strand with a knot.

candied rose petals

you will need

- 8–ounce custard cup
- 2 teaspoons meringue powder
- ¼ cup water
- fork or wire whisk
- cookie tray with rim
- waxed paper
- superfine sugar
- rose petals, whole Miniature roses, or rosebuds (organically grown)
- small paintbrush

pretty tasty

Have fun making these sugar-dusted accents for desserts, tea sandwiches, and hors d'oeuvre trays. Substitute firmly whipped egg whites for the meringue powder and water mixture. If you do, add a couple of drops of vodka to the egg whites after you whip them to help them dry better.

eminently edible

right: Garnish desserts, such as ice cream or cake, with candied rose petals and buds.

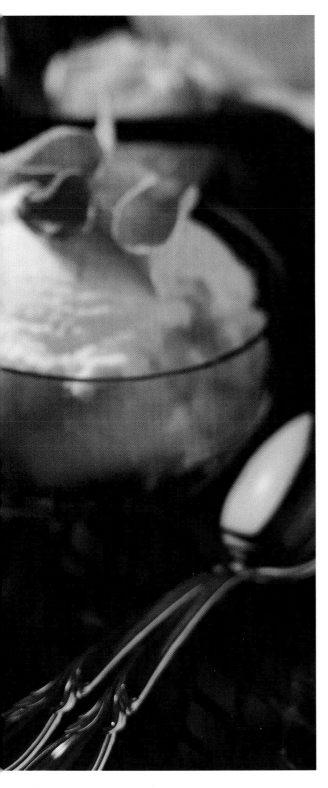

1 stir Combine 2 teaspoons of meringue powder (available at kitchen supply stores) and ¼ cup of water in a clean, dry 8-ounce custard cup. Stir with a fork or wire whisk until the powder dissolves. Set aside.

2 prepare Line a cookie sheet with waxed paper. Sprinkle it with a thin layer of superfine sugar.

Gently pick petals from roses that have just begun to open. Also use rosebuds or whole Miniature roses.

3 coat Rinse rose petals with cold water. Blot them with paper towels and lay them out to finish drying. Use a small, clean paintbrush, such as an artist's brush, to lightly coat the petals or rosebuds with meringue mixture.

4 sprinkle Sprinkle sugar over the petals to coat them evenly. Shake off excess sugar. Place petals on the pan and let them dry overnight in a cool, airy place. If the petals are not used immediately, store them in a covered tin in the refrigerator for up to three weeks.

rosy cooler

rose and raspberry cooler

Make a refreshing, slightly sweet drink by selecting delicately fragrant rose petals, such as 'Cécile Brünner,' *Rosa centifolia muscosa, R. damascena,* 'Double Delight,' *R. gallica,* 'Gertrude Jekyll,' 'Mister Lincoln,' 'Perfume Delight,' *R. rugosa,* 'Tiffany,' or 'Zéphirine Drouhin.' Try different roses each time you make this light, cooling drink and discover which ones have the most aromatic and pleasing flavors.

4   *cups organically grown rose petals, plus more for*
        garnishing (optional)
    2-quart glass bowl
1   *bottle dry white, blush, or sparkling wine*
¼   *cup vodka*
1   *cup fresh raspberries plus more for garnish*
        (optional)
    ice cubes
    sparkling water (optional)
    mint sprigs (optional)

Cut out the yellow or white centers at the base of the rose petals to avoid any bitter taste. In a 2-quart glass bowl, combine the rose petals, wine, vodka, and raspberries; cover and chill for 2 hours. The color of the rose petals and the number of raspberries you use will affect the cooler's pink hue. Before serving, strain the wine mixture; discard petals and raspberries. Serve over ice. If desired, top with a splash of sparkling water and garnish with additional berries, rose petals, or mint sprigs. Makes 6 to 8 servings.

refreshing roses

right: **All rose petals are edible if you grow them without using toxic chemicals. White and pink petals yield the clearest liquid; red petals impart a pinkish tint.**

hip hooray

Let the last roses of summer wither on the plant. This allows roses to begin preparing for winter by developing hips, or berrylike fruits packed with seeds.

Harvest these delectably tart and nutrient-rich seedpods and use them fresh or dried to make jam, jelly, tea, or syrup. Or leave the rose hips on the plants and savor their bright beauty throughout the winter, as long as birds don't eat them all.

Richer in vitamin C than oranges, rose hips have become a valued ingredient in vitamin supplements. They also contain vitamins A, B, E, and K.

Heirloom roses, such as Rugosas, Hybrid Musks, and Species, as well as wild varieties, produce the largest hips. Harvest hips when they're fully colored (red, orange, or purplish) and ripe.

bird food

above: Leave rose hips on the bushes for hungry birds and squirrels to feast on through fall and winter.

spots of color

left: Various sizes of plump, luscious rose hips add color to the garden after the flowers fade.

public rose gardens

Northeast

Elizabeth Park Rose Garden
150 Walbridge Rd.
West Hartford, CT 06119
203/722-6543

James P. Kelleher Rose Garden
Park Dr.
Boston, MA 02130
617/635-4505

Jack D. Lissemore Rose Garden
Davis Johnson Park & Gardens
137 Engle St.
Tenafly, NJ 07670
201/569-7275

Cranford Rose Garden
Brooklyn Botanic Gardens
1000 Washington Ave.
Brooklyn, NY 11225
718/623-7200

Old Westbury Gardens
71 Old Westbury Rd.
P.O. Box 430
Old Westbury, NY 11568
516/333-0048

Hershey Gardens
170 Hotel Rd.
P.O. Box 416
Hershey, PA 17033
717/534-3492

Longwood Gardens
Rte. 1, Box 501
Kennett Square, PA 19348
610/388-1000

Southeast

Bellingrath Gardens Rose Garden
12401 Bellingrath Garden Rd.
Rte. 1, Box 60
Theodore, AL 36582
334/973-2217

Elizabeth Bradley Turner
   Memorial Rose Garden
The State Botanical Garden of Georgia
2450 S. Milledge Ave.
Athens, GA 30605-1624
706/369-5884

American Rose Center
8877 Jefferson-Paige Rd.
Shreveport, LA 71119
318/938-5402

Hodges Gardens
P.O. Box 340, Hwy. 171 S
Florien, LA 71429
318/586-3523 or 800/354-3523

Biltmore Estate
One N. Park Square
Asheville, NC 28801
800/543-2961

Memphis Botanic Garden
750 Cherry Rd.
Memphis, TN 38117-4699
901/685-1566

River Farm
American Horticultural Society
7931 E. Boulevard Dr.
Alexandria, VA 22308
703/768-5700

Midwest

Cantigny Gardens
One S. 151 Winfield Rd.
Wheaton, IL 60187
630/668-5161

George L. Luthy Memorial Botanical Garden
2218 N. Prospect Rd.
Peoria, IL 61603
309/686-3362

Reiman Gardens
1407 Elwood Dr.
Ames, IA 50011
515/294-2117

Frances Park Rose Garden
2600 Moores River Dr.
Lansing, MI 48911
517/483-4223

Lyndale Park Rose Garden
4125 E. Lake Harriet Pkwy.
Minneapolis, MN 55409
612/661-4800

Laura Conyers Smith
    Municipal Rose Garden
Jacob L. Loose Memorial Park
5200 Pennsylvania
Kansas City, MO 64112
816/784-5300

Memorial Park Rose Garden
58th and Underwood Ave.
Omaha, NE 68132
402/444-5497

Stan Hywet Hall and Gardens
714 N. Portage Path
Akron, OH 44303
330/836-5533

Boerner Botanical Gardens
5879 S. 92nd St.
Hales Corner, WI 53130
414/425-1131

Southwest
Historic Saguaro Ranch Rose Garden
9802 N. 59th Ave.
Glendale, AZ 85301
623/939-5782

Tulsa Municipal Rose Garden
Woodward Park, 21st and Peoria
Tulsa, OK 74114
918/746-5135

Fort Worth Botanic Gardens
3220 Botanic Garden Blvd.
Fort Worth, TX 76107
817/871-7686

Salt Lake Municipal Rose Garden
1602 E. 2100 S. Sugarhouse
Salt Lake City, UT 84106
801/467-0461

West Coast
Fairmont Park Rose Garden
2225 Market St.
Riverside, CA 92501
909/7155-3440

Golden Gate Park Rose Garden
Golden Gate Park
San Francisco, CA 94117
415/666-7003

Huntington Botanical Gardens
1151 Oxford Rd.
San Marino, CA 91108
626/405-2100

Northwest
Corvallis Rose Garden
Avery Park
Corvallis, OR 97330
541/766-6918

International Rose Test Garden
400 S.W. Kingston Ave.
Portland, OR 97201
503/823-3636

Woodland Park Rose Garden
5500 Phinney Ave. N
Seattle, WA 98103
206/684-4803

Canada
Minter Gardens
52892 Bunker Rd.
Box 4
Chillawack, British Columbia V2P 6H7
888/646-8377

Niagara Parks Botanical Gardens
2565 Niagara Pkwy.
Niagara Falls, Ontario L2E 6T2
877/642-7275

Royal Botanical Gardens
P.O. Box 399
Hamilton, Ontario L8N 3H8
905/527-1158

sources

Antique Rose Emporium $10.00
9300 Lueckemeyer Rd.
Brenham, TX 77833-6453
800/441-0002
www.weareroses.com

David Austin Roses, Ltd. free
15393 Hwy. 64 W
Tyler, TX 75704
800/328-8893
www.davidaustinroses.com

Forestfarm (C) $5.00
990 Tetherow Rd.
Williams, OR 97544-9599
541/846-7269
www.forestfarm.com

Gardener's Supply Co. (E, O) free
128 Intervale Rd.
Burlington, VT 05401
888/833-1412
www.gardeners.com

Gardens Alive! free
5100 Schenley Pl.
Lawrenceburg, IN 47025
812/537-8650
www.gardensalive.com

Heirloom Roses (M) $5
24062 NE Riverside Dr.
St. Paul, OR 97137
503/538-1576
www.heirloomroses.com

Kinsman Co., Inc. (E) free
P.O. Box 428
Pipersville, PA 18947
800/733-4146
www.kinsmangarden.com

Jackson & Perkins (M) free
1 Rose Ln.
Medford, OR 97501
800/292-4769
www.jacksonandperkins.com

Moore's Miniature Roses (M only) $1
2519 E. Noble
Visalia, CA 93292
559/732-0309
www.miniatureroses.com

Nor'East Miniature Roses (M only) free
P.O. Box 307
Rowley, MA 01969
800/426-6485
www.noreast-miniroses.com

Peaceful Valley Farm Supply (E, O) $3
P.O. Box 2209
Grass Valley, CA 95945
888/784-1722
www.groworganic.com

The Roseraie at Bayfields free
P.O. Box R
Waldoboro, ME 04572-0919
207/832-6330
www.roseraie.com

Smith & Hawken (E) free
P.O. Box 431
Milwaukee, WI 53201-3336
800/776-0431
www.smithandhawken.com

Trellis Structures (E) free
60 River St.
Beverly, MA 01915
888/285-4624
www.trellisstructures.com

Vintage Gardens (M)
2833 Old Gravenstein Hwy. S
Sebastopol, CA 95472
707/829-2035
www.vintagegardens.com

Wayside Gardens (C, E, M) free
1 Garden Ln.
Hodges, SC 29695-0001
800/213-0379
www.waysidegardens.com

USDA Plant Hardiness Zone Maps

This map of climate zones helps you select plants for your garden that will survive a typical winter in your region. The United States Department of Agriculture (USDA) developed the map, basing the zones (Numbered 1 to 11) on the lowest recorded temperatures across the country. Zone 1 is the coldest area and Zone 11 is the warmest.

Plants are classified by the coldest temperature and zone they can endure. For example, plants hardy to Zone 6 survive where winter temperatures drop to −10° F. Those hardy to Zone 8 die long before it's that cold. These plants may grow in colder regions but must be replaced each year. Plants rated for a range of hardiness zones can usually survive winter in the coldest region as well as tolerate the summer heat of the warmest one.

To find your hardiness zone, note the approximate location of your community on the map, then match the color band marking that area to the key.

Hawaii

Australia

United Kingdom

Range of Average Annual Minimum Temperatures for Each Zone

Zone 1: Below -50° F (below -45.6° C)
Zone 2: -50 to -40° F (-45.5 to -40° C)
Zone 3: -40 to -30° F (-39.9 to -34.5° C)
Zone 4: -30 to -20° F (-34.4 to -28.9° C)
Zone 5: -20 to -10° F (-28.8 to -23.4° C)
Zone 6: -10 to 0° F (-23.3 to -17.8° C)
Zone 7: 0 to 10° F (-17.7 to -12.3° C)
Zone 8: 10 to 20° F (-12.2 to -6.7° C)
Zone 9: 20 to 30° F (-6.6 to -1.2° C)
Zone 10: 30 to 40° F (-1.1 to 4.4° C)
Zone 11: Above 40° F (above 4.5° C)

index

index

index

index

photo credits

Rob Cardillo
22 (bottom) 50 (top left) 76 (bottom) 77 (top) 78 (bottom) 123 (top)

Ros Creasy
22 (top) 50–51 (bottom) 73 (center right) 109 116

Saxon Holt
13 16 (bottom) 16 (top right) 18 (top right) 20–21 (bottom) 21 (bottom) 21 (top) 23 24 (top) 24 (bottom) 25 (bottom) 27 (bottom right) 28 (bottom left) 29 (bottom right) 31 33 (left)

34 (top left) 34 (top right) 35 36–37 (bottom) 37 (bottom right) 37 (top) 39 40 (top right) 43 44 (bottom) 45 (bottom) 46–47 (bottom) 48–49 (top) 49 (bottom right) 51 52 (top right) 78 (bottom) 79 93 (bottom) 93 (top) 107 (top right) 111 (bottom right) 122

Dency Kane
11 (bottom right) 46 (top right) 52 (bottom right)

Rosemary Kautzky
18 51 (top) 73 (bottom right) 121 (bottom)

Jerry Pavia
20 (top) 28 (top) 28–29 (bottom) 33 (top right) 38 (top) 38 (bottom) 44–45 48 (top left) 48–49 (bottom) 53 (left) 77 (bottom) 94 (top) 95 (top)

With appreciation to Jackson & Perkins for the rose image on pages 42–43; Hill & Hughes, Portland, Oregon, for the trellis plan illustrated on page 105, illustrated by Roxie Lamoines; and to Fiskars for the soaker hose image, page 67.

metric conversions

U.S. Units to Metric Equivalents

to convert from	multiply by	to get
Inches	25.400	Millimeters
Inches	2.540	Centimeters
Feet	30.480	Centimeters
Feet	0.3048	Meters
Yards	0.9144	Meters
Square inches	6.4516	Square centimeters
Square feet	0.0929	Square meters
Square yards	0.8361	Square meters
Acres	0.4047	Hectaers
Cubic inches	16.387	Cubic centimeters
Cubic feet	0.0283	Cubic meters
Cubic feet	28.316	Liters
Cubic yards	0.7646	Cubic meters
Cubic yards	764.550	Liters

To convert from degrees Celsius (C) to degrees Fahrenheit, (F) multiply by ⁹⁄₅, then add 32.

Metric Units to U.S. Equivalents

to convert from	multiply by	to get
Millimeters	0.0394	Inches
Centimeters	0.3937	Inches
Centimeters	0.0328	Feet
Meters	3.2808	Feet
Meters	1.0936	Yards
Square centimeters	0.1550	Square inches
Square meterers	10.764	Square feet
Square metres	1.1960	Square yards
Hectaers	2.4711	Acres
Cubic centimeters	0.0610	Cubic inches
Cubic meters	35.315	Cubic feet
Liters	0.0353	Cubic feet
Cubic meters	1.308	Cubic yards
Literers	0.0013	Cubic yards

To convert from degrees Fahrenheit (F) to degrees Celsius (C), first subtract 32, then multiply by ⁵⁄₉.